FIRST AND SECOND
PETER

by

GEORGE H. CRAMER

MOODY PRESS

CHICAGO

Printed in the United States of America

CONTENTS

INTRODUCTION

GOD'S PENMAN

THE NEED for a steadfast hope that reaches beyond time and for a knowledge surpassing the noblest of human pronouncements is certainly as great today as in the days of the early Church. The Apostle Peter was a most likely choice as God's inspired penman to deliver these timely messages as found in the two epistles bearing his name. His own personal experiences as recorded in the Gospels are interwoven in all of his writings and the reader seems to sense that his teachings and exhortations come out of a mature and triumphant faith in the Lord Jesus Christ.

Peter had been so sure of himself when he said, "Though I should die with thee, yet will I not deny thee" (Matt. 26:35). But alas, between confession and performance lay the arena of testing; and Peter with cursing and swearing said, "I know not the man" (Matt. 26:74). Luke tells us that Jesus "turned, and looked upon Peter. And

Peter remembered the word of the Lord, how he had said unto him, Before the cock crow, thou shalt deny me thrice" (Luke 22:61). Bitter tears coursed down Peter's cheeks, smarting the weathered face of this former fisherman. But yet more bitter was the remorse of soul as he realized that in time of dire need he had disavowed his Lord and Master.

A door of hope was opened to the apostle after the resurrection. The angel's special instructions were to "tell his disciples *and Peter* that he goeth before you into Galilee: there shall ye see him" (Mark 16:7). The record gives no details but we know that through that open door Peter found restoration and bright hope for the future in the fellowship and service of his risen Lord. His relief in forgiveness and the joy of restoration were precious indeed.

To speak with any certainty concerning the finality of truth as it is in Jesus Christ, only two others could share the honors with Peter—James and John. These three were the Lord's closest disciples. On the mount of transfiguration they were dazzled by the sight of His resplendent glory. They witnessed this certification of all that Jesus said and accomplished during His earthly days.

Thus Peter's faith and the preaching did not

rest upon myth or fable, nor yet upon the wisdom of men, but upon God's own revelation. It is no wonder that Peter was so dogmatic concerning a knowledge of the truth. It is no wonder that such knowledge is prescribed without apology, as the only antidote to vain philosophies and immoral living.

GOD'S PROVISION

To provide a trustworthy source of *hope* and *knowledge* needed for believers of all generations, God needed to create in the recipients an unwavering devotion to His enduring Word (I Peter 1:25).

Peter himself was quite conversant with this Word, and his writings reveal an unquestioned trust in that which God had spoken. The writings of "the prophets" (I Peter 1:10-12) had come alive as the many facets of Messianic prophecy found fulfillment in the person and ministry of Jesus, the Nazarene. To this fulfillment Peter and the other "apostles of the Lord and Saviour" bore witness (II Peter 3:2) because they had associated with Jesus from His baptism to His ascension to the Father's right hand (Acts 1:21-22).

The content and order of events in the life of Christ soon became stylized in the preaching of

the early church. This was the means whereby the
recipients of Peter's two epistles had been brought
to faith in Christ. That faith had been nurtured
by the devoted ministry of the apostles and other
witnesses to the common body of truth concerning the Saviour. But these witnesses could not
effectively continue to perpetuate the message by
word of mouth. Peter, in particular, felt keenly
the need of putting his teachings in a more per-
manent form that they might remain with the
Christians always as a reminder and source of
encouragement (II Peter 1:14-15).

Without question, Peter's two messages were
most timely to the initial recipients. They were
now plunged into doubt and despair by unde-
served suffering, and were ravaged and misled by
smooth operators in their midst. But to consider
these epistles less meaningful and irrelevant for
modern day Christians would be an injustice to
the purposes of a loving heavenly Father.

GOD'S PURPOSE

In the First Epistle

A gem of rare beauty is best displayed against a
dark background, and thus nothing detracts from
its evident worth and splendor. Ominous storm
clouds had gathered, forming a dark backdrop

around these Christians; "the fiery trial" had descended upon them. Then Peter, with deft strokes of the pen, proceeded to set in place the jewel of hope before their tearstained, questioning eyes, "But rejoice, inasmuch as ye are partakers of Christ's sufferings; that, when his glory shall be revealed, ye may be glad also with exceeding joy" (I Peter 4:12-13).

The Apostle Peter, in his ministry to scattered and suffering Christians, was not unlike stouthearted Zerubbabel and Joshua. Nearly six hundred years earlier these two men kept the lamp of hope burning for the fainthearted remnant charged with the rebuilding of Jerusalem and the temple (Zech. 4:3, 14). The apostle's words were most assuring to New Testament believers as they gave open allegiance to Jesus Christ. Such devotion to Him provoked both ridicule and wrath. Ridicule was brought on primarily because they believed in and witnessed to an actual resurrection from the dead. Their testimony incurred wrath because they spoke of this resurrected One as "Lord" and "King," a statement that could not be tolerated by a blinded, monotheistic Judaism nor by a proud cult[1] of emperor worship.

[1] Merrill C. Tenney, *The New Testament* (Grand Rapids: Wm. B. Eerdmans Publishing Co., 1953), pp. 98-99.

Simply stated, the purpose of this epistle was twofold. First, it was designed to orient the Christians to suffering. There was need to understand the reason why suffering had become their lot, and to realize that they were thereby identifying themselves with Christ in His sufferings. Second, there was need to lift their eyes in hope from present, temporal circumstances to future, eternal realities.

In the Second Epistle

A brief span of time had elapsed and the "fiery trials" of Peter's first epistle seem to have abated. Now, rather than arising from outside the church, the threat and cause for concern arose from within. Warning against the subtle and malicious work of false teachers constitutes much of Peter's burden. He knew that the believers had not grown sufficiently in grace and true knowledge. So to the experienced eye of the apostle the threat of false teachers was just as real and present as was the "suffering" of his first epistle.

These false teachers professed much knowledge and yet manifested so little godliness in their lives. It was only to those initiated into their society, the intelligentsia, for whom creation would unfold its secrets which were veiled to the masses. The favored few exalted intellectualism above the revealed truth of God and so despised and cast off the restraints of scriptural commands. This led to a moral breakdown—the inevitable consequence of departure from an authoritative Word of God. In place of faith and love they spoke much of knowledge. The most sacred things of the Christian faith were used as barter to obtain sensual satisfaction as they lusted after personal gain.

The Christians whom Peter addressed had received much instruction in the truths of God. Both through apostolic preaching and by letters the Christian faith had been fully expressed. These believers had no need of further revelation, but there was need to stir up their minds to reflect and act upon what they already knew.

Peter prepared them to receive the teachings of his letter as authorized exhortation (1:12, 15). At least this seems to be his implication in 1:16: "We did not follow cunningly devised fables," and in 1:20-21: "No prophecy of scripture is of private interpretation, for no prophecy ever came by the will of man, but men spake from God, being moved by the Holy Spirit" (ASV). The focal point of their reflection should be the trustworthiness of the Old Testament prophecies.

A second area of concern is not with the trustworthiness of the Scriptures, but with the "things foretold by the holy prophets, and the command of the Lord and Saviour through your apostles" (3:2, C. B. Williams Translation) as concerning the coming of the Lord. Peter believed that this expectation, although delayed in fulfillment, was most needful to the Christian and he set about to underscore these teachings by means of the epistle.

FIRST PETER

First Peter

THE SALUTATION

CORRESPONDENTS in New Testament times crowded a wealth of material into the salutation, even when the message was brief; and Peter, fisherman though he was, followed the accepted style of the day. Herein he gives his name, his calling, the recipients, their privileged relationship to God the Father and his wish for their blessing and spiritual welfare.

The writer introduces himself as "Peter, an apostle of Jesus Christ." No longer is he known as "Simon, son of Jona," but "Peter," the rock, so named by Jesus when He set him apart as an apostle (Matt. 16:18). In the intervening years, by example and by patient teaching, with much forbearance, the Lord had effected His will in the life of this humble fisherman. Now he was indeed a "rock" who demonstrated the power and grace of the exalted Lord.

"The elect who are sojourners of the Dispersion" (1:1, ASV) in Pontus, Galatia, Cappodocia, Asia, and Bithynia [in Asia Minor, contemporary Turkey] were the ones to whom this letter was first directed. Indications are that the epistle was circulated from one group of believers to another in clockwise fashion, beginning in the north by the Black Sea and ending in the north.

Whether or not these congregations were wholly Jewish cannot be determined with finality, but the term "sojourners of the Dispersion" was commonly used to designate Jews who had been scattered (as seed is sown) among the Gentile nations. James, in his salutation, uses the same word for "dispersion" (Greek-*diaspora*) although he specifically qualifies "the twelve tribes" (James 1:1). Peter's use of "Gentiles" in 2:12 and 4:3 adds to the conviction that these Christians were of Jewish stock. It ought not be overlooked, however, that a number of passages, as in 4:3, have implications which are meaningful only if some Gentiles were in the group addressed.

While one need not identify himself with the national or ethnic backgrounds of those whom Peter addresses in order to receive comfort and hope from the epistle, one must stand with them in the ranks of the "elect" if God's message to suffering Christians is to serve its purpose. The nation Israel was God's "elect" or "chosen" people

(Deut. 7:6; Rom. 9:4-5), but with the bringing in of a new covenant through the sacrifice of Christ, God revealed a "choice" or "election" which had been determined "before the foundation of the world" (Eph. 1:4). This elect group is from all peoples and predestined to be "conformed to the image of his Son" (Rom. 8:29).

To clarify the term "elect," Peter uses prepositional phrases as modifiers: (a) it is "according to [*kata*] the foreknowledge of God the Father"—a knowledge which is "part of His eternal counsel" and with "a view to choice and calling",[1] (b) it is "in[*en*] sanctification of the Spirit," whereby the believer is "conformed to the image of his Son" and (c) it is "into [*eis*] obedience and sprinkling of the blood of Jesus Christ" which is foreshadowed in Exodus 24:1-11. According to the latter passage, after the slaying of the oxen, the blood was sprinkled on the altar while the faithful pledged obedience to the Lord; then the blood was sprinkled on the people, which fact identified them as belonging to Jehovah—the covenant-keeping God. The fulfillment in Christ is clearly set forth in Hebrews 9 and 10.

Peter closes his salutation with what is almost a

[1] Edward G. Selwyn, *The First Epistle of St. Peter* (London: Macmillan & Co. Ltd., 1952), p. 119.

prayer, that grace and peace be multiplied to
them. "The Apostle here blends the Western
[Greek] and Eastern [Hebrew] modes of salutation".[2] With the blessings of two great cultures
vouched to them in biblical measure, "pressed
down, and shaken together, and running over"
(Luke 6:38), the suffering Christians were better
prepared to meet the "fiery trials" facing them.

[2] F. B. Meyer, *Tried by Fire* (New York: Fleming H. Revell
Co., n.d.), p. 15.

I

THE REALITY OF HOPE

1:3—2:10

A. GOD'S PROVISION, 1:3-12

EACH GENERATION of Christians has its own unique experience of suffering even as Jesus taught in the Beatitudes, "Blessed are they which are persecuted for righteousness' sake: for their's is the kingdom of heaven" (Matt. 5:10). The antichristian forces arrayed against righteousness today appear in various garbs and with different tactics than those which caused concern and questioning to the suffering Christians of the early church. Yet the best antidote now, as in that day, is a living, vibrant hope in the God who is above *all* circumstances and is known by the believer as the "Father of our Lord Jesus Christ."

While Peter was "musing" on God's provision for these Christians, "the fire burned" (Ps. 39:3); then he too spoke, but not immediately of the things on which he was meditating. His expression was rather one of praise and adoration to the Father for His marvelous provision in the redemptive work of His dear Son. "Blessed" was commonly used to ascribe praise to God. In Zachariah's prophecy in Luke 1:68 "blessed" prefaces a recital of God's marvelous doings in behalf of His people.

1. *Regeneration,* 3-5

The first of God's marvelous works which occasions praise is regeneration. In his praise Peter begins where eternal life begins for the child of God—at the impartation of divine life by the Holy Spirit's ministry. Here, however, focus is not on the Spirit as agent effecting the new birth but upon the resurrection of Christ, the foundation and fountain of all spiritual blessings for the Christian.

From the outset the theme of *hope* is dominant— hope that is not wishful thinking but a living vibrant assurance. The Christian identifies experientially with Christ in death to the flesh and in resurrection into a new and spiritual realm of life. Thus being born of God, into His family, the Christian is now heir to a glorious inheritance. Unlike earthly riches, this inheritance is imperishable, undefiled, and unfailing. These three

words used to describe the inheritance are graphic privatives, with the prefixes negating the positive quality of the words which, taken alone,
characterize only the fleeting things of time.

Because hope finds fulfillment only in reality, it
is not sufficient to present, even with clarity, the
spiritual riches which God in love has provided.
Assurance that the child of God will one day
enter into that inheritance, that there is no possibility of bankruptcy or misappropriation—this assurance is indispensible to hope in times of trial
and suffering.

This assurance is given in a threefold way.
First, the inheritance is "kept" (or reserved) in
heaven for the believer. *Second,* the believer is
"constantly being guarded" here and now to car-
ry him through to the time of his entering into
these riches of heaven. The expression is an old
military term meaning "to garrison." One is reminded of the experience of Elisha and his servant at Dotham (II Kings 6:13-17) when the
unseen army of the Lord of Hosts stood between
them and the enemy. Such protection by the
power of God is experienced "by faith." *Third,*
the Christian is assured that he will be present at
the great "unveiling" when "in the last time" all
the glories of our great salvation will be displayed
for all to behold.

2. *Refinement,* 6-9

Administered in love, refinement is necessary to purify the believer and to establish his faith, unalloyed with doubt.

The *purpose* of refinement (vv. 6-7) is set forth in a context of both joy and sorrow, and each is necessary in the Christian's development just as warp and woof are essential in the weaving of cloth. Although the wonder of our inheritance calls forth rejoicing, there is need of "various trials" for "a little while" (C. B. Williams Translation). Even as gold is refined by fire, causing the dross and impurities to rise to the top for removal, so trials refine the Christian's faith—a much more precious commodity than gold.

The *procedure* of refinement (vv. 8–9) is not concerned primarily with the removal of "dross" from the Christian's life but with the effects on the "inner man," especially on the attributes of faith and love. In the midst of these severe testings, the face of the Refiner becomes visible. Then in wonder and amazement the Christian perceives that the trials are all a part of God's loving plan in redemption. Then the only reasonable response is one of love and submission.

The object of love's response is the Lord Jesus Christ who, though not visible to the eye, is truly present with each believer (John 14:18, 23) and

Peter observes that "having not seen, ye love [Him"]. The outlook of love is faith—"yet believing." Napoleon summed it up well, "An extraordinary power of influencing and commanding men has been given to Alexander, Charlemagne, and myself. But with us the presence has been necessary, the eye, the voice, the hand. Whereas Jesus Christ has influenced and commanded His subjects without His visible bodily presence for eighteen hundred years."[1]

The outcome of love is "unutterable and exalted joy" now in the midst of trials, and as the consummation of a life of faith, the "salvation of your souls." It may seem that Peter implies salvation is some possession merely of the future, but not so. In verse 2 Peter's readers are described as the "elect"; in verses 4 and 5 their inheritance is "kept" for them while they are "guarded" and kept in order to enter into that inheritance. This seems to be a logical order where soul salvation is the result of the exercise of faith, both presently and ultimately.

3. *Reassurance*, 10-12

The ministry of Old Testament prophets contributes much to the Christian's hope, especially

---

[1] Selwyn, *op. cit.*, p. 131.

the many portions which speak of Messiah (Hebrew equivalent for "Christ," meaning "anointed") and His mission. Many of the prophecies had found literal fulfillment in Christ's first coming as Saviour; therefore the believer can, with confidence, expect fulfillment of the remaining promises of Christ's return in glory to establish his reign as "King of Kings, and Lord of Lords" (Rev. 19:16).

The *concern* of the prophets was with "the sufferings of Christ, and the glory that should follow" (v. 11). It was not from utterances of earlier prophets but from their own messages, inspired by "the Spirit of Christ which was in them," that this concern arose—a concern not only to express the message clearly but, more important, to interpret the significance of that message.

Their *consideration* of this theme was manifested both subjectively and objectively. First, it caused them to reach beyond the exercising of their prophetic gift to become not unlike research scholars, seeking out and searching diligently into the significance of their message. It should be noted that the process here is just the reverse of normal communications. The spokesman or writer has the concepts clearly in mind, and uses words which fully and clearly express his thoughts to others. With this communication, under the inspiration of the Holy Spirit, the prophets expressed the mind of God but then were forced to study and search in order to understand the significance.

Objectively, their concern was with "what [time], or what manner of time," not with "what person or time," as in the Revised Standard Version. The Person of their prophecy was not enigmatic but the relative time and the religious and cultural "climate" were not at all obvious. These prophets were seemingly goaded on in their search by the "Spirit of Christ" within them Who "kept on pointing out" (force of the imperfect tense of the Greek verb) this twofold theme, "the sufferings of Christ, and the glory that should follow."

The *conclusion* of the matter may have been a bit disappointing to them. There seems to be indication from the phrase "serving not themselves" (v. 12, RSV) that they hoped it might transpire in their own lifetime. In fact so wonderful is this message that even angels eagerly desired to "peer into" it and indeed did so in a measure as over Bethlehem's plains they praised God for the incarnation (cf. Luke 2:13-14). Fulfillment was not for the prophet's day however but for New Testament saints and primarily for those who heard this message of redeeming grace through the Spirit-filled preaching of the apostles and early evangelists.

B. MAN'S RESPONSE, 1:13—2:10

Having laid the foundation for hope in God's provision, Peter then charges the readers with personal responsibility to God as Father and to other believers as fellow-heirs of eternal life. If the preceding section were to be classified as "doctrinal," then this section places emphasis on the "ethical" demands which naturally follow.

1. *An Exhortation*, 13-25

"Wherefore" introduces a series of inferences, describing the expected response to God's marvelous provision. This response is seen in purity of life and in perfection of love.

To purity of life, 13-21. The apostle's purpose in writing this epistle seems to be set forth in verse 13, a bolstering of their hope which should be fully and completely focused on the day of revelation of Jesus Christ. Then faith becomes sight; things hoped for, actuality.

This kind of hope (a verb in the form of a command) is to be perfectly focused on the end results of God's grace. Herein is victory and steadfastness for the Christian. It is not enough simply to "desire" a hope which overcomes all obstacles. A sluggish, earthbound mind will defeat the best desires, falling short of reality.

Therefore the exhortation is "gird up the loins of your mind." This vivid metaphor was most forceful to the recipients who often had seen men tuck the ends of their long, flowing garments into a wide belt or girdle at the waist so as not to be impaired in running. Picture Elijah, if you will, with his long robe tucked into his girdle, running before the chariot of Ahab to the gate of Jezreel as the long-awaited rain began to drench the parched earth (I Kings 18:42-46). The mind, playing a vital role in the cultivating of purity, is to be likewise "girded."

The Apostle Paul realized the role of the mind in developing Christian character. In Romans 12:2, renewing of the mind brings about a transformation (metamorphosis), and in II Corinthians 10:5 "bringing into captivity every thought to the obedience of Christ" is necessary to wage successful warfare against the flesh. In this cultivation of inward purity, the grace of God is not overlooked but there is the outworking of that which has been wrought within the believer manifested in holiness and reverence.

Holiness, even as our God and Father is holy!

How awesome and seemingly out of reach. And so it is to anyone, except the child of God who follows the new compulsion of obedience to the will of God. There is no longer a continuing in the former habits and paths, characterised by "lusts" (or passions) and "ignorance." These refer to the manner of life before the Christians were "begotten . . . anew to an ever living hope" (v. 3, William's Translation).

Now rather than "fashioning" themselves according to the old pattern of life, a new standard is set forth, doubly binding because of the calling and the commandment to be holy (Lev. 11:14). It might well be countered that New Testament saints have received the imputed righteousness or holiness of Christ and what Christian does not take comfort from this transaction. But Peter is pressing here for a holy life which demonstrates to all the grace of God within.

Second, reverence is called forth from the Christian's heart by the thought of God's righteous judgment. Unlike men, He judges not according to outward appearance. How well Peter had learned this lesson in the vision of a sheet containing all manner of beasts, fowl and creeping things. This truth was indelibly etched on his soul two days later—for God visited the household of Gentile Cornelius with the "like gift" of salvation given to the Jews.

Recounting this experience, Peter said, "Of a truth I perceive that God is no respecter of persons" (Acts 10:34). As He imparts salvation, so He judges. It thus behooves the heirs of salvation to walk carefully before Him.

What a shame it is that some are so attached to this transitory life that complete purity in God's sight is not desired. They are in bondage to sin. The price of redemption has been paid, yet they are unconcerned. And a greater price has never been paid to redeem one from bondage. Costly metals from the earth would not suffice; but the precious life blood of God's Son fully satisfied the ransom demands. The word for "ransom" is *lutroō*, as ransom paid for a slave (cf. Matt. 20:28).

What a wealth of sacrificial significance! What an unveiling of God's love and personal concern for each redeemed one! The blood of God's Lamb (John 1:29) was more precious, more dear and costly than any blood offered on Jewish altars of old. Because God gave His Son as a ransom, we can begin to understand the value God places upon an individual soul.

The believing child of God is ransomed from the empty and fruitless life of a pagan background (v. 18) to a condition wherein God is uppermost in thought and trust (v. 21). This new outlook is a marked contrast to the previous mode of existence. The new life was planned before creation and effected by the resurrection of Christ and His ascension to a place of power and glory at the Father's right hand. Contemplation of this marvelous provision will certainly call forth the desired response—purity of life.

To perfection of love, 22-25. The purity of life to which Peter had given exhortation, is not to be lived and enjoyed in isolation. It must be expressed to others. It must be shared, and love is the overt expression of holiness or purity of life. The one who has purified his soul by obedience to the truth of God is to love the brethren without hypocrisy and with his whole heart.

This kind of love is possible only because God has implanted a new life within the Christian, "born anew" of the imperishable Word of God. As the nature of the seed, so the nature of the plant which springs forth. The good seed of divine life is implanted by the word which the apostles preached and which Paul sums up in I Corinthians 15:3-4, "Christ died for our sins according to the scriptures; and that he was buried, and that he rose again the third day according to the scriptures."

2. *A Realization,* 2:1-10

New life is realized and evidenced by growth. This is axiomatic in the plant and animal kingdom and is also true in the spiritual realm. Growth is both qualitative and quantitative.

By qualitative growth, 1-3. "Food" is an absolute necessity for growth and "this food for babes in Christ is the Word, which is taken by the Spirit and offered a nurture for the soul."[2] A contrast is seen in verses 1 and 2 between the *husks* (malice, guile, hypocrisies, envies and evil speaking) and the "pure, spiritual milk" which the newborn babe is exhorted to "desire" (a word denoting *intense yearning*).

Why, some may question, must Peter exhort that spiritual babes long for this spiritual baby food? Should this not be as natural and regular as hunger pangs? Undoubtedly it should be a normal response, freely expressed and fully satisfied; but there is a conflict of appetites as implied in verse 1, and those appetites which characterize and sustain the old nature must be denied so the new nature may develop within. Only thus can the new life be expressed.

There is also the possibility that the babe in Christ may desire the "meat" of the Word, but

[2] J. Rawson Lumby, "The Epistles of St. Peter," *The Expositor's Bible* (New York: A. C. Armstrong & Son, 1908), p. 64.

this is for those who are more mature (Heb.
5:12-14). "Milk" answers to the basic teaching of
the faith (Heb. 6:1-2; I Cor. 3:2), while "meat"
refers to the weightier matters and deeper in-
sights into the truths of God. (In Hebrews the
"meat" was applied to teachings regarding the
high priesthood of Christ.) Thus, both physically
and spiritually, solid foods cannot be digested
and are harmful to infants.

By quantitative growth, 4-10. The figure of
speech shifts somewhat, both in nature and comprehension. No longer is the human body and the
individual used, but now the picture is that of a
stone edifice with all believers as stones comprising
the edifice.

Temples are usually monuments of grandeur to
the spectator. But the eye of a skilled craftsman
enjoys detail, observing not alone the obvious
symmetry and charm but scrutinizing the foundation, the quality and shape of stones, the grade
and use of wood, the workmanship with which all
are fitted together. These and an added multitude
of details go into the construction of a beautiful
temple, though unseen and unappreciated by the
untrained eye.

As Peter wrote these words, the fabulous Temple of Herod was being completed (64-65 A.D.). It
was begun in 20-19 B.C. and the temple proper

was completed in one and one-half years and the
courts and cloisters required eight additional
years. In John 2:20 we learn that construction was
still in progress during Jesus' teaching ministry
and was to continue for approximately thirty-six
years.[3] This, then, was the temple that served as a
mental pattern for understanding the figure of the
spiritual temple.

How is this "spiritual" temple built, and of
what materials? The foundation is of prime im-
portance and in 2:7 Jesus Christ is referred to as
the "head of the corner" in fulfillment of God's
promise to Israel (Ps. 118:22; Isa. 28:16). He is
also "a living stone" whom God, not man, has
established as the rock on which to build.

"This 'spiritual house' includes believers in the
five Roman provinces of 1:1 and shows clearly
how Peter understood the metaphor of Christ in
Matt. 16:18 to be not a local church, but the
church in general (the kingdom of Christ)."[4]
These "living" stones (v. 5) are thus built upon
the Living Stone (v. 4) who is the Foundation (I
Cor. 3:11). They partake of the life of the Living
Stone, evidencing corporate growth as other new

[3] James Orr (ed.), "The Temple," International Standard
Bible Encyclopaedia (Grand Rapids: Wm. B. Eerdmans Publishing Co., 1947), V, 2937.

[4] Archibald T. Robertson, Word Pictures in the New Testament (Nashville: Broadman Press, 1933), VI, 96.

"stones" are bonded in by the Spirit of God. (See also I Cor. 3:16; Eph. 2:22; Heb. 3:3-6.)

A twofold purpose—Godward and manward—is served by this spiritual temple. First, the priestly ministry functions on the vertical plane (Godward) as the believer-priests offer "spiritual sacrifices" to God. Some biblical sacrifices are: one's body (Rom. 12:1), praise (Heb. 13:15), doing good (Heb. 13:16) and sharing with others (Phil. 4:18). Such sacrifices are effective and acceptable to God only as mediated by our Great High Priest—Jesus Christ (v. 5). On the horizontal plane (manward) the Christians are instructed to "shew forth [tell out] the praises" of God who called them "out of darkness into his marvelous light." Thus in a twofold manner is this priestly ministry fulfilled.

God's sovereign choice in the corporate design of this "spiritual house" is abundantly evident. Even though the foundation stone was rejected by the "builders" (the leaders in Israel), God's purposes overruled. Jesus Christ has been established among men as a touchstone of faith and obedience. He is a divider among the people. To those who believe, He is "precious"; to the disobedient, He is a "stone of stumbling" and a "rock of offence" (2:7-8).

By noting God's design we do not conclude

that God ordains man's perdition, but that it is
ordained by man's own disobedience. On the
other hand, those who esteem Him "precious" are
an "elect *[chosen]* race, a royal priesthood, a holy
nation, a people for God's own possession"
(ASV). With God thus working according to His
own purpose in grace, Christian *hope* becomes a
bright and blessed reality when evidenced by
growth.

II

THE RATIONALE OF HOPE

2:11—4:11

It has been said that a Christian can see further on bended knees than can a philosopher on tiptoes. Perhaps this saying contains an element of truth that has direct bearing on the rationale of hope. Many experiences in the Christian life, whether ordinary or traumatic, do not belong to a pattern of life formulated and directed by reason alone. But submission to the will of God produces experiences which provide a foundation for a *rationale of hope* and demonstrate "that good, and acceptable, and perfect, will of God" (Rom. 12:2).

There are four avenues of appeal for submission—*command, conscience, cognition* and *compact*—and all four demand a hearing from the Christian.

A. SUBMISSION—THE IMPERATIVE OF COMMAND,
2:11—3:12

The imperative of command recalls to mind the
awesomeness of God's presence on Sinai at the
giving of the law (Exodus 20:19) and how the
Hebrews desired that Moses communicate God's
law to them rather than have God speak directly.
Whether attended by thunderings and lightnings
or by the clarity and authority of an inspired
Word, God's commands should be honored and
obeyed.

1. *In Personal Relationships*, 11-12

Submission to God must be demonstrated in
personal relationships before it can be manifested
to others. Quite appropriately, purity of life, ad-
vocated by warnings against fleshly lusts, is
presented as an indirect command, before the
direct commands of 2:13, 2:18, 3:1 and 3:8 are
given. This indirect command is bolstered not by
a threat but by a heartfelt entreaty from the
apostle—"I beseech." Purity of life should not be
an unbearable yoke because the ones addressed
are already spiritual "strangers and pilgrims"
(RSV—"aliens and exiles") to the world order and
its lustful pursuit of pleasure. And conversely,

these strangers in the world are "fellow citizens
with the saints" (Eph. 2:19).

These "fleshly lusts which war against the soul"
are not delineated but in general can be described as follows: "Lust is inordinate desire—the
desire for *too much* of a good thing, or for *any* of
a bad thing."[1] One is reminded of Abraham's
conduct in the midst of heathen peoples (Heb.
11:13-16). (Although the words used in verse 13
are not identical with those used by Peter, yet
there is little difference in the meaning.) When
Abraham put his confidence in God's promises, he
was kept from entangling alliances in the land of
his sojourn (vv. 14-16).

There is also a positive aspect to Peter's entreaty. As the fruit of submission to God's will, "good
deeds" (RSV) become very convincing in the
presence of godless and evil men. In fact, it is
expected that some who see the grace of God thus
demonstrated will turn in faith to God and will
glorify God "in the day of visitation" for working
through His children.

The "day of visitation" may seem a bit ambigu-
ous, especially if we attempt to interpret it as an
end-time event. In this context, the most obvious
approach seems to be the most appropriate, that

[1] Howard W. Ferrin, *Strengthen Thy Brethren* (Grand
Rapids: Zondervan Publishing House, 1942), p. 75.

is, the day when God visits them with forgiveness and salvation. Then, looking back, they will remember and thank God for the example of Christlikeness which, as signposts, marked their path leading to salvation.

2. In Civic Relationships, 13-17

The imperative of command, "submit yourselves," now focuses on the Christian in society. There may be justification for crusading against the wrongs in government and society; in fact, scriptural injunctions may be marshaled in support, but these verses could not contribute to the case. For that matter the opposite seems to be true.

Keep in mind the historical context out of which this epistle arose. The Christians were undergoing persecution for their faith and often these trials were provoked, or at least condoned, by the Roman authorities. In such a social context, "we ought to obey God rather than men" (Acts 5:29) would have been very inappropriate as a response. Rather than honoring God and fulfilling His purpose in witness-bearing, such an approach would have been abortive, to say the least. Excellent illustrations which Peter could have used here are the stories of Joseph and of the four Hebrew servants in heathen courts (Gen. 37-45; Dan. 1-6).

It is both a privilege and a responsibility for God's "free men" to be submissive to every "human institution" (RSV) for "the Lord's sake." Peter begins with submission to the emperor (v. 13) and concludes with the charge to give him honor (v. 17). Roman emperors were certainly not kindly disposed to Christians; in fact, just the opposite was true. Outward circumstances are quite incidental in the discharge of one's civic responsibility because it is "for the Lord's sake," not the sake of the individual.

3. *In Servile Relationships,* 18-25

That the Christian servant is commanded to serve may appear somewhat paradoxical and may seem to be unnecessary if the servant is truly Christian. But these "household servants" had been purchased, not by good and gentle masters, but by "the crooked" householders. (The same word is used to describe the generation of Jews who rejected their Messiah and Saviour [Acts 2:40]; Paul also applies this word to unbelieving Gentiles among whom the Philippian Christians lived [Phil. 2:15.])

"The absence in I Peter of any injunctions to slave-owners (contrast Col. 4:1) suggests that there were no Christian slave-owners among the people to whom the letter was originally ad-

dressed."[2] Even so, though little consideration
was shown them, submission is the Christlike
approach to servitude (Mark 10:45). According
to custom, the Christian slave could save up and
purchase his freedom, but until the emancipation
he was bound before God to be an obedient
servant. Hence, verse 18 describes the scope of
submission.

The spirit of submission follows in verses 19 and
20. Responding "in kind" is ruled out when the
servant suffers unjustly at the hand of an ungodly
master. Such submission is deadly to pride but
quickening to the Christian's conscience. However, submission to just punishment for a misde-
meanor is not at all praiseworthy.

Having instructed the servant to submit for
the sake of his Christian testimony, Peter now
presents the Saviour as the classic example of
suffering unjustly (vv. 21-25). The word for example, *hupogrammon*, has two classical uses,
"(1) a 'tracing' of letters for children to write over
or to copy" or "(2) an architectural outline or
artist's sketch, to be coloured or filled in by others."[3] Both meanings contribute to our understanding of Christ as an example of suffering

---

[2] Edward A. Maycock, *A Letter of Wise Counsel* (London:
Lutterworth Press, 1957), p. 61.

[3] Edward G. Selwyn, *The First Epistle of St. Peter* (London:
Macmillan & Co. Ltd., 1952), p. 179.

unjustly. A few "tracings" or "sketches" of our great Example should suffice.

Christ's attitude, which controlled both word and deed, is certainly noteworthy and the Christian is called to manifest a like attitude under trial. All the more wonderful it is when we know that He suffered unjustly. He had not sinned or wronged any one, yet He was mocked, cajoled, spit upon, smitten and crowned with thorns. He bore all the mistreatment patiently, committing His case to the Righteous Judge—His Father—for vindication.

His accomplishments (vv. 24-25) likewise challenge the Christian to submit to God's will under trial because through Christ's submission many have been made righteous and have been brought into the fold (John 10:1-18). Here Christ is presented as both Sacrifice and Shepherd to the Christian who places his trust in Him. Lacking assurance of sins forgiven and of the lordship of Christ to guide and to protect, one cannot bear reproach and mistreatment in doing what is right.

4. *In Marital Relationships*, 3:1-7

Down through the ages those who have held to a biblical view of creation and of the institution of marriage realize the wonder of Adam's statement (Gen. 2:24), "they shall be one flesh." Equally

significant and relevant in this "enlightened" age
is God's word to woman after the transgression:
"Thy desire shall be to thy husband, and he shall
rule over thee" (Gen. 3:16). Oneness in the marital bonds and man's position as head of the home
constitute the two God-ordained pillars which
support marriage.

Because of these two pillars, the Apostle Peter
spoke a word to both parties concerning responsibilities as Christians in the home. His exhortation
to the woman is more detailed and lengthy than
to the man, perhaps because her role is more
difficult to maintain, being subservient and yet a
fellowheir of the grace of life. Or perhaps it may
be that more exhortation was needed because of
the practices of heathen women who, predomina-
ting in the fashionable circles in that Greco-
Roman world, may have lived as neighbors to the
women whom Peter was addressing.

The wife's responsibilities, 1-6. A basic ingredi-
ent of a happy marriage is the wife's submission to
her husband. This certainly stands in marked
contrast to pagan marriages where a wife was
regarded as the property of her husband, and was
treated with little or no consideration. The apostle's concern here is for the home and because
every institution must have a head to function
smoothly and effectively, the wife must give def-

erence to the husband who is the head. In I Corinthians 11:3, the Apostle Paul touches on this very matter, "the head of every man is Christ; and the head of the woman is the man; and the head of Christ is God." To maintain this divine order, submission to headship is not only desirable but necessary.

Chastity is also essential to a happy marriage (v. 2). Many have been the occasions when unbelieving husbands have been repelled rather than attracted to Christianity by the preachments and forwardness of a zealous, yet inconsistent, wife. A submissive, Christlike spirit is lauded as the most effective means of winning a nonbelieving husband. The word translated "conversation" in verses 1 and 2 is the Greek word *anastrophe* and refers to the total behavior pattern. If anyone is in a position to observe this conversation it is certainly the husband.

A classic example of a wife's wordless evangelistic efforts is St. Monica. Her son St. Augustine gave testimony to her life: "When she came to marriageable age, she was bestowed upon a husband and served him as her lord, and she did all she could to win him to Thee, speaking to him of Thee by her deportment, whereby Thou madest her beautiful and reverently lovable and admirable to her husband. . . .Finally, when her husband was now at the very end of his earthly life, she won him to Thee."[4]

The third necessity is modesty (vv. 3-5) which is encouraged first by contrast and then by example. Certain negative exhortations were essential as a background for contrast. Practices of dress and adornment, carried to excess, were not unknown to the Christians of that day. Much attention to the pursuit of physical attraction is well expressed in the word *kosmos*, translated "adorning" (from which *cosmetic* is derived).

This meticulous care was lavished on coiffures, jewelry and dress. Roman coiffures were very elaborate, braided and worn tier upon tier. The populace took avid interest in hair styles, expressing choice by poll or voting. It has been said that women were afraid to sleep soundly at night lest the coiffure be spoiled. But Scripture teaches that a pleasing appearance, dependent only upon that which is outwardly applied, is not real beauty.

In positive exhortation, Peter would have the godly woman understand that true beauty originates in the "hidden man of the heart." And "a meek and quiet spirit" is a jewel most precious (v. 4). This text does not teach that attention to

[4] Aurelius Augustinus, *The Confessions, Basic Writings* (Ed.) Whitney J. Oates (New York: Random House Publishers, 1948), I, 139.

external adornment is wrong. Of course not, but
when that attention becomes the primary concern, or the only concern, it is a snare and a
delusion to the Christian, "for it is character that
really matters, and character is of the heart."[5]

Beauty and modesty are not mutually exclusive
as illustrated by the example of Sarah (vv. 5-6).
Whether or not her example is seriously considered, either in the first or in the twentieth century, is a matter not of contemporaneity but of
relationship. Sarah is considered mother of all
those who hope in God and recognize the headship of the man in the marital bonds.

The husband's responsibilities, v. 7. The exhortation to husbands is short indeed by contrast. Two
possible reasons are that the Christian husband
was not confronted with the same spiritual prob-
lems in the marital bonds as was the Christian
wife married to a pagan man. It has also been
noted that men were in the minority in the early
Christian communities.[6]

The husband must "live considerately" (RSV)
with his wife, not dominating as "head of the
house" nor yet venting his whims and passions at

<hr/>

[5] Maycock, *op. cit.,* p. 66.
[6] Francis Wright Beare, *The First Epistle of Peter* (Oxford:
Basil Blackwell, 1947), p. 131.

will because she is the "weaker vessel." A husband will find his greatest satisfaction in the marital state by recognizing that he and his wife share a common lot as heirs together of God's grace.

5. *In Brotherly Relationships,* 8-12

The portion opens with "finally," not with intent to conclude the epistle, but to terminate exhortations to the several groups addressed in this portion (2:11–3:12). Not one among them was excluded from this exhortation. Stranger or citizen, slave or freeman, husband or wife—all were in the brotherhood of believers by faith in Christ and as such shared mutual family concerns.

The calling of the Christian (vv. 8-9) is to oneness of heart, mind and deed even as Christ is one with the Father in His eternal purpose and program (John 17). Peter uses three adjectives, not used elsewhere in the New Testament, to describe Christians' attitudes one to another. The Christians whom he addressed knew full well the force and meaning of these terms.

Christians were to be "like-minded," not imitators one of another, but always seeking the mind of Christ. They were to be characterized by "sympathy" or "compassion" (perhaps better, "empathy"). The third word used to describe the Christians means "loving the brethren."[7]

In addition, Christians were to be tenderhearted, humble-minded and, in general, characterized by brotherly relationships. After such pointed exhortations, there was still need to underscore certain actions which are not compatible with brotherly love. Retaliation should have no part in the Christian's attitude or conduct, regardless of what others do.

The "blessing" (v. 9) is promised to those who live in accordance with the Christian graces given in verses 8 and 9. As support, Peter quotes from Psalm 34:12-16. These were not unfamiliar words to those originally addressed, especially since many were Jewish in background (cf. 1:1). The Psalms were sung by the Jews in worship, so many of these portions from the Psalms early found their way into the Christian hymnody and catechetical instructions. The point is that God's blessing rests upon those who speak and do righteousness, but His disfavor is upon those who practice evil.

B. SUBMISSION—THE IMPERATIVE OF CONSCIENCE, 3:13-22

The second avenue of appeal for submission is

---

[7] *Ibid.,* pp. 133-34.

the believer's conscience. Obligation imposed by command cannot produce the desired response any more than could the law of Moses justify a devout Israelite before a holy God. There is need for an unlocking of man's will, for stimulation of right desires, if one is to respond to God's commands for righteous living. Of all man's faculties, conscience exercises the greatest influence on the soul.

1. *From a Christian Attitude,* 13-17

The question, "And who is he that will harm you, if ye be zealous of that which is good?" (v. 13, ASV) is provoked by the last line of the quotation, "The face of the Lord is against those who do evil" (v. 12). It should be inferred that the Christian who is zealous for God is so surrounded and safeguarded that neither harm nor reproach can get through to him. (See Daniel 3:19-27.) The believer can be touched by nothing that is not the will of God, even though suffering *is* sometimes God's will for His own (cf. 2:19-21 and 3:16-17).

The apostle encourages the Christian to be zealous for righteousness by making three things clear: normally, one does not suffer harm and mistreatment for doing good; if there be the rare exception (expressed by a conditional sentence which indicated little likelihood) to this general principle, then the sufferer is truly blest of God, and "happy." (See Matthew 5:10 where the same word is used.) And the Christian, thus armed with confidence, should neither fear nor be troubled by the evil workers.

Peter goes on to speak of the Christian's convincing witness. When Christ is sanctified or enthroned as Lord in the heart, the issues of life whether spoken or acted out will be imbued with a sense of His presence. Thus emboldened, the Christian is prepared to give an "apology," or "a reasoned defense," of the hope he has in Christ. This to the unbeliever may seem nebulous and fanciful, but to the believer, clear and assuring. The apostle does not imply that the carper or evildoer will be won thereby to faith in Christ, but that a reasoned defense of the Christian's faith is not only possible but potent in conviction when given in humility.

The convincing witness is given by godly living as well as by word of mouth. "Good behavior in Christ" (RSV) will put to shame the evildoers who seek to bring reproach upon the follower of Christ. For this good behavior one is sometimes called upon to suffer.

2. *From Christ's Example*, 18-22

The second appeal for submission is by example, pointing to Christ who without sin of His own became a sin offering in our behalf. This passage is without doubt the most difficult to interpret of all Peter's writings, primarily because, departing from exhortation, he becomes involved in a deep and somewhat figurative Christological discourse. A wide variation in standard commentaries on this passage is ample evidence of the problem. Most of the views would with some possible modifications fall under one of the following interpretations: (1) The Spirit of Christ was in Noah while he built the ark and preached righteousness; (2) It refers to the story of Enoch, in the apocryphal book bearing his name, where he in spirit preached to the spirits in prison; (3) Christ in His preexistent state preached to those who had rejected Noah's preaching and who are now in prison; (4) It refers to Christ's ministry, in spirit, between death and resurrection.

His humiliation, 18-21. In the midst of an attempt to unravel the tangled threads of this difficult passage, the reader should not lose sight of the major thread of truth joining it to the larger context. Peter speaks of submission as being the imperative of conscience and he illustrates this from the proper Christian attitude and from

Christ's own example. This example is described in a threefold way, portraying the manner, the motive and the means of His humiliation.

The manner and the motive are briefly stated and are introductory to the third which presents the Christological problem mentioned above. Christ's suffering even unto death speaks of the manner of His humiliation, "the just for the unjust." His death was not by accident but by divine purpose and design. Thus the motive is "that he might bring us to God."

The means of His humiliation can be stated very simply, "being put to death in the flesh, but made alive in the spirit" (ASV). Alford has expressed this idea well: "His flesh was the subject, recipient, vehicle, of inflicted death: His spirit was the subject, recipient, vehicle, of restored life. . . .He, the God-man Christ Jesus, body and soul, ceased to live in the flesh, began to live in the spirit; ceased to live a fleshly, mortal life, began to live a spiritual resurrection life."[8]

The problem of interpretation lies not in this portion quoted from verse 18 but in the modifying portions immediately following. Linguistically interpreted, only one meaning is admissable as to the time and form of His preaching "to the spirits

[8] Henry Alford, *The Greek New Testament* (Chicago: Moody Press, 1958), IV, 364-65.

in prison." The time seems to be circumscribed by His "being put to death in the flesh" and His ascension to "the right hand of God". The form is "in which [spirit] he went and preached."

This ministry has been confessed by the church for centuries in the so-called Apostle's Creed, (though challenged by some) "he descended into hell," or more accurately, "Hades." "The Greek word 'Hades' translates the Hebrew word 'Sheol', which was the place to which the spirits of all people were believed to pass at death; there they waited until the final judgment; 'Hades' must not be confused with 'Gehenne', the place of the lost."[9] The word used for "prison" is not specialized but the common word used for a place of incarceration, as a Roman prison (Acts 16:23) or the "bottomless pit" from which Satan shall be loosed for a little season (Rev. 20:3-7).

What was the purpose of his preaching to the "spirits in prison"? Perhaps if their identity could be clearly established, the purpose would not be so difficult of solution. Some of the more common identifications by biblical scholars are: 1) the people of Noah's day who heard the "spirit" of Christ preaching through Noah; 2) the fallen angels, as in Jude 6-7, who had been imprisoned

[9] Maycock, op. cit., p. 73.

for disobedience; 3) the spirits of those who did not heed Noah's preaching of coming judgment and were imprisoned in "Hades."

The last identification seems to be the clearest and requires no manipulation in word meaning or in syntax. If thus identified, what is the significance of preaching? What of the results? Peter uses not the word for "preaching the good news of salvation" but a word which simply means "to announce" or "to herald," without revealing the content of the message.

In the unseen realm Christ's death had many far-reaching effects which stagger the imagination. Why these particular individuals in Hades were singled out for a proclamation by the Son of God is not clear. Perhaps an answer may be found in the typical use of Noah's preaching of impending judgment and of salvation provided in the ark. Herein full redemption by Christ was prefigured, and yet to this message Noah's contemporaries had closed their ears. In Christ, the patriarch's message had been verified and fulfilled.

Concluding the example of Christ's humiliation, Peter introduces baptism which has been suggested by his reference to Noah's family having been saved "through water" by the ark. "Peter jumps from the flood in Noah's time to baptism in

Peter's time, just as he jumped backwards from Christ's time to Noah's time."[10]

Undoubtedly, he refers to water baptism which was used by the Apostle Paul to symbolize identification with Christ in death and resurrection (Rom. 6:3-4). The washing is not to effect outward cleansing, as in Judaism or as in pagan religions, but to consummate and to make visible man's part in the work of regeneration (cf. Mark 16:16; Acts 2:38.) However, Peter makes it quite clear that without the resurrection of Christ, baptism is ineffectual and meaningless.

His exaltation, 22. As the incarnation was God's method of clothing His Son with humility, so the resurrection was His method of releasing Christ from the last of all human experiences—death. The *right* hand of God, a place of honor and esteem, speaks of the position of His exaltation. His power is unquestioned because "angels and authorities and powers" have been made subject to Him.

The significance of this exaltation is seen not in relation to baptism and the need for a good conscience, but in relation to His death and resurrection as His means to "bring us to God" (v. 18). The Christian can be assured that his redemption

[10] Archibald T. Robertson, *Word Pictures in the New Testament* (Nashville: Broadman Press, 1933), VI, 118.

will be consummated; nothing can now separate
him from the love of God in Christ (Rom. 8:38-
39).

C. SUBMISSION—THE IMPERATIVE OF COGNITION, 4:1-6

The third avenue of appeal for submission is
cognition which can function only in the life that
has identified with Christ in death and in resurrection. Suffering in the flesh because of sin—not
His own—is a finished transaction and requires no
repeating: "Christ . . . suffered for sins once [for
all]" (3:18, ASV). "Arm yourselves with the same
thought" is Peter's exhortation to those who were
already suffering but who lacked understanding
of the reason or yet of its liberating consequences.
Cognition of this marvelous provision is experienced by reckoning and reflecting on the applica-
tion of Christ's suffering to Christian experience.

1. *By Reckoning*, 1-2

Reckon, as used in the New Testament, directs
a challenge to the will or mind of the Christian.
Here as in the epistle to the Romans the believer
is to reckon himself one with Christ, in death to
sin and all its allurements. This is commonly
called identification with Christ. When he

suffered in the flesh on Calvary it was on our behalf and the believer is exhorted to enter by faith into that same relationship to the life of the flesh as our Substitute experienced when He cried, "It is finished." This speaks of deliverance from previous relationships and motivation, and liberty to pursue all that pertains to eternal life.

The Apostle Paul refers to this identification also as co-crucifixion with Christ (Gal. 2:20). When the Christian is thus "armed" he is prepared to do spiritual battle against foes both without and within. Thus he demonstrates to all "what is that good, and acceptable, and perfect will of God" (Rom. 12:2). *Co-crucifixion* then leads to sharing with Christ in His triumph.

2. *By Reflecting*, 3-6

Just as reckoning leads to identification so reflecting opens the door to sanctification. Entering this open door, the Christian finds his feet in "the path of the just" which is likened to "the shining light, that shineth more and more unto the perfect day" (Prov. 4:18). In this stage of submission, worldly friends are no problem because they are the ones who decide to part company.

Reflection first takes account of the wicked and debased life from which God in grace has delivered us (v. 3). "Will of the Gentiles" stands in marked contrast to the "will of God" in verse 2, and seems to characterize the debauchery of those who live only for self. Because the believer has forsaken this "wild profligacy" (v. 4, RSV) the old companions in sin not only part company but heap abusive language upon the defector from their ranks. (The word used is *blasphēmeō*, from which blasphemy is derived.) Judgment, not blessedness, awaits all such.

The term "the quick and the dead" as it relates to judgment (v. 5) introduces another passage bearing a certain likeness to 3:18 and one which has yielded also to many and varied interpretations. While God is "Judge of all" (Heb. 12:23), yet He has ordained that His Son should exercise judgment regarding man's response to the offer of redemption (cf. Acts 10:42; II Tim. 4:1).

"This phrase *the quick and the dead* was perhaps already semicreedal"[11] so the interpretation need not be exhaustive to do justice to Peter's statement. After a rather thorough survey of the many interpretations (including material in Essay I) Selwyn says, "It is simpler, indeed, to suppose that St. Peter in verse 5 has in mind past and present members of the Church and their

11 Archibald M. Hunter, *The Interpreter's Bible,* (New York and Nashville: Abingdon Press, 1955), XII, 136.

persecutors, and in verse 6 the first of these only."[12]

The gospel provides the challenge and provision for self-judgment (4:1) by identification with Christ—a process of judgment which must span the life "in the flesh" and consummates at physical death. Judgment in the flesh is then set forth as the prelude to living "in the spirit like God," (v. 6, RSV), and this is the common lot of believers.

D. SUBMISSION—THE IMPERATIVE OF COMPACT, 4:7-11

Compact is the fourth avenue of appeal for submission, thus concluding the rationale of hope. This is not an agreement obligating Christians to certain responsibilities. The compact is not written and has no signatures, but it is equally as binding. It has both horizontal and vertical dimensions—outward toward fellow believers and upward toward God.

Furthermore, a sense of urgency pervades this compact because "the end of all things is at hand." In other words, the Lord's return is imminent, both for judgment and reward. One who cherishes this hope conducts his affairs with a

[12] Selwyn, *op. cit.*, p. 214.

view to eternity's values. In marked contrast to verse 3, he has neither time nor desire for drunkenness ("be ye sober") but disciplines his thinking for a more effective life of prayer.

Concern for fellow believers is seen in a threefold use of "one another," (RSV). In verse 8, the concern is for an attitude of love toward one another; in verse 9, it is hospitality to one another; and in verse 10, the exhortation is to use one's God-given gifts for one another. This kind of compact can be displayed only through a common love and a consecrated life.

1. *Through a Common Love,* 7-9

Effective service, whether in prayer or any other ministry, must rest upon the "primacy of love." With the exercise of "fervent" love the Christian community is strengthened and personal differences, even friction and injured feelings, are laid aside. "Love covers a multitude of sin" (RSV) even as the sprinkling of blood on the "mercy seat" (on the ark of the covenant) covered sins of the Israelite in days of old. What a grand demonstration of discipleship when Christians love one another (John 13:35). In such a spiritual climate, hospitality is a part of the daily routine, affording opportunities for fellowship as well as for service to others.

2. *Through a Consecrated Life,* 10-11

God gives gifts to His children, not primarily to make them happy, but to use them as channels and hands of His omnipotence. The days of Christ's earthly ministry came to an end at Calvary. Now, "as good stewards of God's varied grace" (RSV), as "ambassadors for Christ" (II Cor. 5:20), believers minister to the glory of God. Every area of life, every effort expended, should be toward this end because He alone is worthy.

III

THE REWARD OF HOPE

4:12—5:11

Earlier in chapter 4 (vv. 5, 7) a solemn note is sounded, warning of imminent judgment. In this closing portion of the epistle, judgment is also mentioned (4:17), but the picture is not dark and ominous; beyond the suffering and trials there is glory (4:13; 5:4), and beyond the humiliation, exaltation (5:6).

Even as hope is a reality in the midst of suffering (See Section 1.), so the reward of hope is equally assured with the "inheritance . . . kept" in heaven for the believer, and the Christian is "garrisoned about" so as to endure and survive for entering into that reward (1:4-5). Reward, in the New Testament, usually refers to the completed product, e.g. the crown of life, the crown of glory, crown of rejoicing, crown of righteousness, and the incorruptible crown. In this portion of I Peter, reward is promised for spiritual stamina in service and in strife.

A. For Fortitude of Soul, 4:12-19

It seems quite obvious that with verse 12 we leave behind the broad principles of Christian life and witness before a pagan world, and localize our thoughts to a "particular community—with the distress and terror occasioned by an actual persecution."[1] The soul is fortified for those withering blasts of trial and persecution if the Christian is aware that suffering with Christ is corollary to believing. (See Phil. 1:29.) Then with confidence the believer can commit his soul to a loving and faithful Creator.

1. *With Glory in Suffering,* 12-16

A very basic principle of human experience serves as context for these exhortations. One may be taught the ways of man, both pleasant and distasteful, but he never anticipates or realizes the significance of the distasteful experiences until they are thrust upon him. Likewise the Christian may know about suffering for Christ but the searing yoke is rarely welcomed. In fact such an aspect of the fellowship with Christ is usually foreign to the Christian and comes as a great surprise.

[1] Francis Wright Beare, *The First Epistle of Peter* (Oxford: Basil Blackwell, 1947), p. 162.

By way of preparation, Peter exhorts, "Stop thinking that [the testing] . . . is a thing alien to you" (v. 12 Wuest's Expanded Translation). God proposes, through this refinement, to burn off the dross so that the pure "gold" may remain (this metaphor used in 1:7). Rather than being fearful and troubled, the Christian should "rejoice" in being counted worthy to share in Christ's sufferings. Thus, sharing in His sufferings, he also shares in His glory in that future day when Christ is revealed in resplendent glory as King of kings and Lord of lords. Suffering reproach for the name of Christ should only strengthen the believer and verify his stand on the truth.

In verse 15, Peter lists a number of misdemeanors worthy of punishment, but makes it clear there is no merit in suffering itself. If one who calls himself a Christian is punished for his misdeeds, he has received his just deserts. However suffering for truth, for a just cause ("as a Christian"), is no occasion for shame before fellowmen. Rather it is an occasion to glorify God by humbly accepting whatever He sends.

2. With Grace in Judgment, 17-19

The thought of judgment beginning with God's people is not new, in fact in the vision given to Ezekiel, the most hallowed spot received first consideration: "Begin at my sanctuary" (Ezek. 9:6). Selwyn says of I Peter 4:17-19 that "two ideas are combined in these verses: (1) that the divine Judgment begins at the house of God, an idea expressed by our Lord in the concrete action of the Cleansing of the Temple, (2) that it is already operative in the trials suffered by the Christian community."[2]

Since there is need for judgment among God's people and inasmuch as it receives primary attention, what hope is there for those who spurn God's grace? The apostle supports this line of reasoning by a quotation from the Greek (Septuagint) version of Proverbs 11:31, indicating that it is with "difficulty" (through great trials and afflictions) that the righteous are eventually "saved."

Therefore, the Christian should be resigned to suffering now, "according to the will of God" as a part of God's grace in redemption because such suffering purges from sin and delivers one from God's wrath in the last judgment. Thus the Christian is exhorted to "entrust" (as deposit in the bank; cf. I Tim. 1:18 and II Tim. 2:2) his soul to a "faithful Creator" as One who is all-powerful and all-loving. In this the Christian follows the example of the Saviour who, expiring on the cross,

[2] Edward G. Selwyn, *The First Epistle of St. Peter* (London: Macmillan & Co., 1964), p. 226.

said, "Father, into Thy hands I commit my spirit" (Luke 23:46).

B. FOR FAITHFULNESS IN SERVICE, 5:1-7

As the epistle draws to a close, the content becomes increasingly personal. Leaders and people alike must be faithful in discharging their responsibilities despite the adverse circumstances surrounding them.

1. *To Shepherds of the Flock,* 1-4

The elders here were ministers or shepherds, having oversight of the church. The basis of the apostle's appeal is that he is a fellow elder, (v. 1). No one is quite so capable, because of personal experience, to give these exhortations as Peter. In addition to being one with them in responsibility and burdens as a fellow elder, his credentials are further enhanced by the unique experience of being a witness (Greek—*martus,* from which our word "martyr" is derived, because in death the martyr "bore the supreme and unanswerable testimony"[3] to his faith) to the sufferings of Christ and a sharer, in "the glory that shall be revealed."

The context gives no indication as to when or how this unique experience took place, but without doubt it rests upon Christ's three and one-half

[3] Beare, *op. cit.,* p. 172.

years of ministry consummated in His ascension,
and Peter's bold declaration of the evangel (cf.
Acts 2:36; 4:10-12). Ministering as witness for
Christ he had shared in a measure the suffering
and glory of His exalted Lord.

The burden of the apostle's appeal is under-
girded by personal experience, indelibly etched
upon his heart and implicit in the exhortation,
"Tend the flock of God which is among you" (vv.
2-3, ASV). Could Peter ever forget his denial of
the Master (Matt. 26:74), the Lord's look of compassion (Luke 22:61), the assurance of forgiveness
from the risen Christ and the charge to be a
shepherd of the flock (John 21:15-19)?

Then out of his own experience he exhorts the
shepherds by three couplets in vivid contrast: 1)
Concerning one's heart, service should be "not by
constraint, but willingly"; thus, shepherds cannot
be coerced to care for the flock; 2) concerning
one's mind, service must not be "for filthy lucre,
but of a ready mind"; that is, one should not serve
with wages or personal gain as the primary objec-
tive; 3) concerning one's bearing, shepherds
should be humble examples to the flock and not as
"lords [domineering] over God's heritage."

The benediction of his appeal rests in that hope
common to Christians all ages—the coming of
Christ in power and great glory (v. 4). In that

day when He rewards His saints, the faithful shepherd will receive an unfading crown of glory. Crowns or wreaths of honor were in common usage in New Testament times, with perhaps the most common use being that of the award to the victor in the Greek games. The wreaths (often made of laurel) soon withered. But the crown given by the Chief Shepherd will be "unfading," a word derived from "the name of a flower *amaranth* (so called because it never withers and revives if moistened with water and so used as a symbol of immortality)."[4]

2. *To Sheep of the Fold,* 5-7

This exhortation to the "younger", in contrast to the "elders" (v. 1), is not to be construed as designating official rank, but age. All the younger ones were to be in subjection to the leadership of those more mature. Their responsibility was twofold—to the elders, and to God.

The *elders* deserved not only a hearing but also respect because of the wealth of experience and knowledge they had acquired. Certainly this is not a new emphasis. Abundant examples can be found in the patriarchal economy in Old Testament days. Personal relationships are not to be

[4] Archibald T. Robertson, *Word Pictures in the New Testament* (Nashville: Broadman, 1933), p. 132.

characterized by sham and hypocrisy. But God expects each Christian to "clothe" himself with humility. One can find no greater example of humility than Jesus' washing His disciples' feet (John 13). Here Peter learned with amazement that He whom he had confessed as the "Christ, the Son of the living God" would stoop to a servant's ministry.

Because *God* gives grace to the humble, the Christian's safeguard against fightings without and fears within is submission to the Father's perfect will, wherever and however it may lead. This is certainly not an evidence of weakness as the Marxist philosophy would have us believe, but humility in the divine order has been and always will be a prelude to honor (Matt. 5:3; Luke 18: 9-14).

Since "it is a care to Him" what transpires in the life of each believer, the exhortation is "Cast all your anxieties on Him" (RSV). This includes past memories, present difficulties, and future fears. What a welcome invitation in the midst of contemporary pressures; yet, how difficult to experience fully! Thomas Baird has set forth this struggle so clearly in these lines:

It is His will that I should cast
My care on Him each day,

> He also bids me *not* to cast
> My confidence away.
>
> But oh! How foolishly I act,
> When taken unaware,
> I cast away my confidence
> And carry all my care.

C. FOR FEALTY IN STRIFE, 5:8-11

Trials and testings often come through the agency of everyday surroundings—people, things, circumstances. But the discerning Christian sees behind these visible, tangible sources of trial. He sees the Master Mind of all evil—the one who empowers, directs and uses these natural means to frustrate the grace of God. Lest a suffering saint misconstrue the source, Peter declares plainly that the Christian's adversary is the "devil" and the only way to overcome in the strife is by fealty (faithfulness) to the "God of all grace."

1. *Toward the Strategy of the Adversary*, 8

It behooves the child of God to be on the alert always and in every place because he is involved in a spiritual warfare against a real, not an imaginary, foe. Peter here identifies him as *diabolos* (devil), the Greek counterpart of the Hebrew name "Satan." In addition to these two names

(Satan and devil), he is also known in Scripture by many descriptive titles, each signifying a certain aspect of his evil work. Here he is called the Christian's adversary.

Because he thwarts God's will in the believer more by fear than direct intervention, the devil is appropriately called "a roaring lion." Not that direct encounter is never experienced (Job 1-2), but more often fear is a most effective tool in accomplishing his ends. He is characterized as "prowling" around, seeking someone "to drink down" (literal meaning).

2. *Toward the Strain of the Conflict,* 9

Part of the Christian's armor in Ephesians 6 is "the shield of faith," designed "to quench all the fiery darts of the wicked." In the conflict with things both real and imagined, faith always dispels fear. By taking one's stand in simple faith, believing that God will protect and vindicate His own, the Christian can thereby resist the devil.

While going through such experience, one should remember that he is not alone in the conflict. All those in the household of faith (Greek, "your brotherhood") experience the same trials. In the midst of trial Peter is saying, "Remember you are not singled out, but the same experience of suffering 'is required' (RSV) of all Christians."

3. *Toward the Song of Victory*, 10-11

Compared with the glory which God has prepared for His saints, any suffering one is required to endure for Christ's sake is only for a "little while." It is significant that Peter uses the title "God of all grace" (cf. 4:10) to characterize the One who, working through these experiences, will "restore, establish, and strengthen" (RSV) the suffering Christian.

His calling, although now momentarily to share in the sufferings of Christ (Cf. 2:21) is but preparation and a brief interlude in the path to eternal glory with Christ. This then, the end product of suffering, is the purpose of God's calling. Thus the Christian can say with the Apostle Peter, "To him be glory and dominion for ever and ever." Implicit in this note of praise is the fact that God is sovereign, and is able to perform all that He designs; therefore the believer can remain faithful and steadfast in the midst of the spiritual battle.

IV

CONCLUSION

5:12-14

In conclusion, Peter sends greetings, summarizes his burden of the epistle, and bestows a benediction. Silvanus (Silas) was without doubt Peter's scribe for this communication; both shared in the concerns for the suffering Christians.

"She that is in Babylon" (ASV) also sends greetings by means of the letter. As to identification, two sets of alternatives confront us: the Church or Peter's wife; Babylon (in Mesopotamia) or Rome—spiritual Babylon. The "coelect woman" could be applied to the church but "the natural way to take it is for Peter's wife."[1]

As to the point of origin for this letter, Rome is more likely than actual Babylon. If Peter wrote during Nero's persecutions, which is very likely,

[1] *Ibid.*, p. 135.

then his use of the symbolic name for Rome (Rev.
17-18) can be readily understood. A careful study
of the facts of the case leads one "to conclude that
the epistle was composed in Rome."[2] Mark,
his son in the faith, also joined in sending greetings.

The burden of the epistle is the declaration that
this, which he has written, is the true grace of
God. There is also the admonition to show affection and esteem one for the other by a holy kiss.
Indication in writings of the early church fathers
is that the use of a kiss as a form of greeting and
affection was abused. In *The Apostolic Constitu-
tions* this admonition is found: "Let the men give
the men, and the women give the women, the
Lord's kiss."[3]

With a priceless bequest he closes the letter—
"Peace be unto you." One is reminded of the Lord
Jesus Christ who appeared to His disciples after
they had shut the doors for fear of the Jews, and
said, "Peace be unto you" (John 20:19). This,
then, is God's gracious ministry to His suffering
saints.

[2] Merrill C. Tenney, *The New Testament* (Grand Rapids:
Wm. B. Eerdmans Publishing Co. 1953), p. 364.

[3] *Ante-Nicene Christian Library,* Alexander Roberts and
James Donaldson (eds.) (Edinburgh: T. & T. Clark, 1870),
Vol. XVII, Book II, Section VII, p. 85.

SECOND PETER

Second Peter

SALUTATION, 1:1

I. KNOWLEDGE AND PROGRESS FOR THE CHRISTIAN, 1:2–11

A. GOD'S PROVISION, 1:2–4
1. Its Certainty, 2
2. Its Comprehension, 3
3. Its Character, 4

B. MAN'S RESPONSIBILITY, 1:5–11
1. As Commanded, 5–7
2. As Contrasted, 8–9
3. As Confirmed, 10–11

II. KNOWLEDGE AND PROFESSION OF THE APOSTLE, 1:12–21

A. TESTIMONY OF A RETIRING MESSENGER, 1:12–15
1. Ministry in Person, 12–14
2. Ministry by Proxy, 15

B. TESTIMONY OF AN EYEWITNESS, 1:16–18
1. Negation—Not in Fables, 16
2. Affirmation—An Historic Event, 17–18

C. TESTIMONY OF AN INSPIRED RECORD, 1:19–21
   1. Certification of the Record, 19
   2. Trustworthiness of the Record, 20–21

III. KNOWLEDGE AND PRETENSE BY THE FALSE TEACHERS, 2:1–22

   A. THE PROGRAM ANALYZED, 2:1–10a
      1. Their Presence, 1a
      2. Their Position, 1b
      3. Their Persuasiveness, 2–3a
      4. Their Perdition, 3b–10a
   B. THE PHILOSOPHY SCRUTINIZED, 2:10b–19
      1. Spiritually Insensitive, 10b–13a
      2. Sensually Incited 13b–16
      3. Subtilely Impelled, 17–19
   C. THE PENALTY SUMMARIZED, 2:20–22
      1. The Predicament, 20
      2. The Proposition, 21
      3. The Proverb, 22

IV. KNOWLEDGE AND PERCEPTION THROUGH REVELATION, 3:1–18a

   A. CERTITUDE OF GOD'S SPOKEN WORD, 3:1–7
      1. By Reflection, 1–2
      2. By Reaction, 3–4
      3. By Recount, 5–7

THE SALUTATION

This epistle was written shortly after the writ-ing of I Peter and obviously, from the salutation, by the same author—Simon Peter. Although II Peter was not readily accepted by the early church, personal references and experiences men-tioned in the letter would support a common authorship for both.

As in his salutation of the first epistle, Peter refers to himself as an "apostle" of Jesus Christ, but also says that he is a "servant" (*doulos*). In this treatise on knowledge, Peter thought it neces-sary that his readers know of his calling and of his being an "eyewitness" (1:16) to three and one-half years of ministry.

Those addressed seem to be the same Chris-tians who, in the first epistle, were enduring great suffering for their faith. These people seem to be suggested in 3:1 with the reference to this treatise as the "second letter."

Their characterization as having "obtained like precious faith" (1:1) with the apostles may have reference to the fiery trials which had tested their faith to burn out the impurities and dross (I Peter 1:7). Hence, their refined faith was akin to that which the apostles possessed because they too had suffered for their faith in Christ, who is both "God" and "Saviour."

I

KNOWLEDGE AND PROGRESS FOR THE CHRISTIAN

1:2-11

A. God's Provision, 1:2-4

Peter had anything but complimentary remarks for the false teachers who had undermined the confidence and dedication of the saints by professing a knowledge and enlightenment available only to a favored few. Perhaps the most devastating result of their teaching was breakdown in proper conduct and morals because a serious question had been raised regarding the authority of God's revelation. Peter countered this by presenting the superior knowledge (*epignōsis*—an intensified form of the word for *knowledge*) which God bestows upon His own.

1. *Its Certainty, 2*

The apostle's earnest desire is that believers be forewarned and fortified against the stratagems of deceivers working in their midst, so he introduces his prayerful concern on which he elaborates in the remainder of the epistle.

Experientially, God's provision for His children is assured to each believing heart by an abundant supply of grace and peace, the substance of the apostle's prayer for them. Grace and peace should not be considered a customary, stereotyped greeting, although it is common in the epistle.

Considering the subtleties and persistence of the false teachers, the grace of God in ever increasing measure was necessary for establishing Christians steadfast in the true faith (3:18). Peace served not only as a common bond, joining Christian to Christian in the cause of truth and righteousness, but also as a guardian of the redeemed soul (3:14). The standard of God's giving as seen in this wish is multiplication; the source is the "superior knowledge" of the true God and of His Son, Jesus Christ our Lord.

2. *Its Comprehension, 3*

"All things" necessary "to foster the spiritual life and to guide into the way of holiness"[1] have been provided graciously by His divine power. Thus the weak are made strong, the fainthearted

---

[1] J. Rawson Lumby, "The Epistles of St. Peter," *The Expositor's Bible* (New York: A. C. Armstrong & Son, 1908), p. 239.

encouraged, the erring forgiven and the poor in spirit made rich with the untarnished wealth which only knowledge of the true God can bestow.

And it is "by" Christ's own "glory and virtue" that sinful man is led to acknowledge his sins and to receive the life that comes only from God. John the Apostle referred to this (John 1:14) when he said that, "we beheld his glory, the glory as of the only begotten of the Father, full of grace and truth." This was the magnetic attraction by which Christ drew apostles to Himself and which has been repeated, generation after generation.

3. *Its Character*, 4

God's provision is climaxed in this verse by a description of the provision's character which influences both natures, new and old. It is difficult to determine grammatically which part of the preceding verse this thought modifies, whether it is to be taken with the "all things" or with the "glory and virtue." On this scholars differ, but it seems more logical to choose the former and thus the "precious and exceeding great promises" (ASV) are given with the "all things."

More important to the Christian, however, is the assurance that these superlative promises have been given, and that they minister to knowledge and progress in Christlikeness. God's promises are of the very essence of spiritual life.

Job, out of a deep longing to know God better and to understand His dealings said, "I have esteemed the words of his mouth more than my necessary food" (Job 23:12). And Peter, suddenly awakened to the absolute necessity of spiritual sustenance, said "Lord, to whom shall we go? Thou hast the words of eternal life" (John 6:68). To Job, Peter and David—to all who have experienced God's Word as a "lamp" for the feet, and a "light" to the path—the promises are indeed "precious" and "exceeding great." These lines of a prayer express it well:

> O may these holy pages be
>   Our ever new delight.
> And still new beauties may we see,
>   And still increasing light.

The New Testament sets forth two ways whereby the child of God becomes a partaker of the divine nature, that is, shares in God's holiness. Chastisement is one method, even though not a very palatable one to the flesh (Heb. 12:10). The second method is appropriating the spiritual equipment and provisions contained in the promises God has given in the Word. This is accomplished through the ministry of the Holy Spirit.

Promises have spiritual substance and meaning only as they lead the believer into a dynamic relationship with the One giving the promises and with His inexhaustible resources. Thus maintaining this vital bond, the passions and habits of the old nature slough off and characteristics of the new nature have opportunity to become established in life and character. This transforming experience is most graphically presented in contrast by the Apostle Paul in II Corinthians 3:15-18.

B. MAN'S RESPONSIBILITY, 1:5-11

After contemplating God's provision for believers, the apostle entreats each Christian to strive diligently for cultivation of these spiritual virtues which, being manifested in the redeemed life, will stand as demonstrable evidence of one's calling and election by God. This requires active participation by the individual, using all things His divine power has provided, and in this demonstration no place is provided for those of faint heart or slothful spirit. The Christian, having received salvation as the gift of God, is called upon to "work out" the spiritual graces of his salvation "with fear and trembling" (Phil. 2:12). In the verses following, man's responsibility is commanded, contrasted and confirmed.

1. *As Commanded,* 5-7

Peter's command that they supplement their faith, giving all diligence to the effort, is not out of keeping with what we know of the apostle. His zeal was often misguided, but he was certainly wholehearted in his efforts to speak and act for the disciples. Response to the slightest opportunity to please his Lord was quite spontaneous and certainly sincere, although not always in the best judgment. He could not be passive in his love and devotion to Christ.

With the same earnestness and urgency Peter would have Christians add to the foundation (faith) which they already possessed from their call into this fellowship (v. 3). This list of graces to be built into the Christian life is called "Peter's golden chain of Christian virtues."[2] However, they may be more aptly described as steps or building blocks, with love as the capstone (cf. Rom. 5:3-5; Gal. 5:19-23; I Thess. 1:3).

To faith the seven graces are to be supplied as one supplies or equips a chorus (from *epi-*

[2] R. C. H. Lenski, *The Interpretation of the Epistles of St. Peter, St. John and St. Jude* (Columbus, Ohio: Lutheran Book Concern, 1938), p. 268.

choregeo). Certainly it does not strain but enhances the meaning of the context to understand that the end result of this supplying is beauty, harmony and enrichment of soul. Some would see here the metaphor of building, banking or growth; but Peter gives no indication other than that which is implicit in the verb *epichoregeo*.

Jowett seems to comprehend the meaning, referring to this effort as "the expansion of our spiritual traffic, to the enrichment of our souls, and the enlargement of our spiritual stock."[8] It can be stated with confidence that it is "in the righteousness of our God and Saviour Jesus Christ" (prepositional phrase modifying "faith" in v. 1). Thus the graces would add qualitatively to the believer's spiritual life.

Although Peter begins his scale or stock of graces with *virtue*, this is not necessarily the first grace that the babe in Christ develops. Some logical relationship may be inherent, and certainly virtue, moral power or vigor of soul, is basic to the developing of Christian graces. *Knowledge* gives insight and understanding, and unless a vigorous faith is directed by knowledge, presumption results.

Next is *temperance* or self-control, without

[8] J. H. Jowett, *The Redeemed Family of God* (New York: George L. Doran Co., 1906), p. 230.

which many men of great promise have ship-
wrecked a life of effective service. Thus control
over the activities within the soul is most necessary. Control in the midst of circumstances without is provided in the grace of *patience*. *Godliness*
refers to a reverence or respect for spiritual
things, thus making the Christian more godlike.

Nothing so demonstrates to the world the reality of Christian profession as *brotherly kindness*, or
affection. The heathen commented of the early
Christians, "Behold, how they love one another,"
and John, the apostle of love, constantly exhorted
the same. But the capstone or crown of all graces
is *charity*, or love, without which all others would
pale to insignificance. (Cf. I Corinthians 13:13
and I John 4:16, 20—a few of the many uses of
agapē, the loftiest form of love known to man.)

2. *As Contrasted*, 8-9

Jesus said, "Wherefore by their fruits ye shall
know them" (Matt. 7:20). Peter adopts the concept by setting forth in sharp contrast two classes
of people, distinguished by their fruitbearing.
Fruit can indicate either the kind of tree (as in
Matt. 7:20) or the health of the tree, as in this
context. The spiritual plant with roots deeply
anchored in faith and nurtured by the seven
"graces" in overflowing measure (cf. Luke 6:38)

will be productive in fruit characterized by and displaying the full knowledge (*epignōsis*) of the Lord Jesus Christ.

On the other hand, he who lacks this cultivation and growth is blind (a word indicating extreme nearsightedness, not total blindness, so as to require a squinting of the eyes to see even near objects), "screwing up his eyes because of the light."[4] If such a one were granted a place with Moses on Mt. Nebo, nothing in the land of promise would be discernible to him. He is unable even to recall the joy experienced when the burden of sin was lifted and he started on his pilgrim journey.

3. As Confirmed, 10-11

This contrast should constrain the sincere believer to assiduously follow the exhortations of verses 5 and 8 that he may have no doubt concerning his position "in Christ." "Even Christians are prone to forget the pit from whence they were digged, the bottom rungs of the ladder by which they have climbed, the solid events of history to which their faith is anchored."[5] Reflecting on all

[4] Archibald T. Robertson, *Word Pictures in The New Testament* (Nashville: Broadman Press, 1933), VI, 152.

[5] Elmer G. Homrighausen, *The Interpreter's Bible* (New York and Nashville: Abingdon Press, 1955), XII, 179.

that God has done should cause the Christian to follow His bidding diligently and thereby demonstrate to himself and to others the reality of his call and election. No ceiling of visibility can obscure hope regarding the reality of the eternal state.

II

KNOWLEDGE AND PROFESSION OF THE APOSTLE

1:12-21

Admissible testimony in establishing any case can be either oral or written, and Peter as a skilled barrister is marshaling all the facts in his case against the false teachers at work in their midst. The witnesses he calls forth possess irrefutable knowledge because of personal experience and God's own stamp of approval.

A. TESTIMONY OF A RETIRING MESSENGER, 1:12-15

Peter was keenly aware that most of his ministry was history. Responsibility for a continuing witness to these Christians weighed heavily upon his heart. Because of this burden he not only determined to continue a personal ministry while living but also to write out an account of his experiences so the addressees (and yet unborn generations) would have a full transcript of his defense of the faith.

1. *Ministry in Person*, 12-14

It should have been comforting news indeed that the apostle's personal concern for their spiritual welfare would not wane during the remainder of his days. Even though they were established in the truth which had been made known to them up to that time, there was need to reiterate the teachings lest the memory dim and the precious truths lose their spiritual dynamic. "Preachers and churches may seem to be saying the same old things repeatedly, *ad nauseam,* but there is no other way to keep the Christian faith alive. This is so because the memory is capricious. We remember a hurt but we forget a favor."[1]

The apostle uses the same word for "establish" that Christ used in command to him in Luke 22:32: "*Strengthen* thy brethren." Peter probably had this in mind. As well, the remembrance of the suffering in I Peter probably prompted him to speak of being "established in the present truth."

Peter senses the nearness of death, not a peaceful "falling asleep" at a ripe old age but a violent death (by crucifixion with head downward, according to tradition) even as Jesus foretold (John 21:18-19). Yet he speaks of his departure, "I must put off this my tabernacle," as calmly as Longfel-

[1] Elmer G. Homrighausen, *The Interpreter's Bible* (New York and Nashville: Abingdon Press. 1955), XII, 178.

low does of daily cares, saying that they "shall fold up their tents like the Arabs, and as silently steal away, ("The Day Is Done"). Hence he was pressed with a feeling of urgency regarding ministry to the saints.

2. *Ministry by Proxy*, 15

Varied interpretations have been given as to how Peter intended to provide a means whereby the believers could recall "these things" after his "decease." One view is that he intended to write other letters. Another view is that he had in mind Mark's gospel which was written by Mark from Peter's personal knowledge and experience. Perhaps a more accurate view is that Peter referred to the contents of this epistle. It is certainly a strong apology for the true faith. Most of his defense, more than two-thirds of the epistle, is yet to be written. "His readers need only reread these chapters at any time, and thus 'effect for themselves the recollection of these things.'"[2]

B. TESTIMONY OF AN EYEWITNESS, 1:16-18

1. *Negation—Not in Fables*, 16

This witness begins by anticipating the response of some, especially the pseudoprophets, to

[2] R.C.H. Lenski, *The Interpretation of the Epistles of St. Peter, St. John and St. Jude* (Columbus, Ohio: Lutheran Book Concern, 1938), p. 289.

the amazing experience he is about to relate. Herein Peter also has a word for many today who would distort and demean the historicity of the gospel records. These critics substitute allegory and myth as a *modus operandi* for exegesis. But Peter's witness relates what he, in company with two fellow apostles, saw and heard on the mount of transfiguration (Matt. 17:1-9). He was not playing the role of a sophist, peddling cleverly fabricated tales of deception to bolster his case. One is reminded of the "Jewish fables" (Titus I:14) to which the Apostle Paul alludes, having in mind "the legends of the Talmud, the subtleties of the rabbinical teaching, and the allegorising interpretations of Philo."[3] The reader of such accounts is hard pressed to distinguish fact from fiction.

The doctrine which occasioned the controversy was the power and coming of our Lord Jesus Christ which Peter had communicated to them as the believer's hope (I Peter 1:7). In this hope they rested, especially in times of persecution and hardship, because their reward was not material and temporal. It was spiritual and eternal and would become actual when Christ returned for His own.

[3] J. Rawson Lumby, "The Epistles of St. Peter," *The Expositor's Bible* (New York: A. C. Armstrong & Son, 1908), p. 263.

The word "power" is quite clear but "coming" (*parousia*) allows for several interpretations. Here, as elsewhere in this epistle (3:4, 12) the word obviously refers to the second coming of Christ. This interpretation is confirmed by use of *parousia* in nonbiblical writings of that period. It "served as a cult expression for the coming of a hidden divinity, who makes his presence felt by a revelation of his power, or whose presence is celebrated in the cult." Or it was also "the official term for a visit of a person of high rank, especially of kings and emperors visiting a province.[4] To this manifestation of Christ as Lord and King, Peter was an eyewitness.

2. Affirmation—An Historic Event, 17-18

A witness is one having personal knowledge of the matter under consideration and Peter attests to the reality of that scene on the "holy mount" when Christ was transfigured in awesome splendor.

The "bright cloud" (Matt. 17:5) probably corresponds to the shekinah cloud of the Old Testament manifestation. Not only did sight attest that dramatic scene but hearing also. There came a voice bearing a twofold witness to Christ:

[4] William F. Arndt and F. Wilbur Gingrich, *A Greek-English Lexicon of the New Testament* (Chicago: University of Chicago Press, 1957), p. 635.

that He was indeed God's Son, His well-beloved; and that with the Son He was well pleased. The term "Majestic Glory" (ASV) is used as an ascriptive title for God.

C. TESTIMONY OF AN INSPIRED RECORD, 1:19-21

Peter introduced himself as both a retiring messenger and an eye-witness. He now undergirds the facts to which he has borne witness with the Messianic pronouncements of the Old Testament which find fulfillment in Christ.

1. *Certification of Record, 19*

Received in faith, God's Word needs no authenticating signs to the trusting soul. Yet time and again God has graciously accommodated Himself to man, the sentient creature, for strengthening of faith and fulfillment of His purposes. The transfiguration scene to which Peter bore witness validated the prophecies of kingship (cf. Matt. 16:28, as an introduction to that which transpired; II Peter 1:16—"majesty"). The testimony of the Father, "This is my beloved Son" could leave no doubt regarding Christ's deity (Matt. 17:5). Thus prophecy is the lamp lighting the way to Christ and also illuminating the many facets of His person and work. Such dependable words serve as the daystar in the heart of believ-

ers, announcing imminency of the coming day
when faith will give way to sight.

2. *Trustworthiness of Record*, 20-21

These two verses are classic references in a
study of the doctrine of inspiration. It must be
clearly understood that Peter referred to the initial giving of the revelation *to* man, not the interpretation of the message *by* man. This understanding of the passage is supported by use of the
word *ginomai,* meaning "comes to pass" or "has its
source" (not "is" as in most translations), and by
idia epilusis, "private interpretation." The verb
epiluō used here means "to unloose, or release." It
is used only twice in the New Testament, in Mark
4:34 where it means "to disclose" the meaning of
a parable, and in Acts 19:39 where the meaning
is "to settle, or decide."

Verse 20 might be translated, ". . . no prophecy
of the scripture has its source in a private dis-
closure." Thus "it is the prophet's grasp of the
prophecy, not that of the readers that is here
presented, as the next verse shows."[5]

Prophecy did not come "by the will of man,"
which is an accurate translation of the Greek

[5] Archibald T. Robertson, *Word Pictures in the New Testament* (Nashville: Broadman Press, 1933), VI, 159.

word *thelēma*. By interpretation however it is quite clear that Peter meant "impulse" (RSV) or "whim" (New English Bible), or to paraphrase, "it did not originate with man." However, as instruments or mouthpieces of God, men spoke from God as they were moved, or borne along, by the Holy Spirit. A message thus given was wholly God's word.

"Peter is not here warning against personal interpretation of prophecy as the Roman Catholics say, but against the folly of upstart prophets with no impulse from God."[6] Peter takes his place with the inspired prophets as a witness to the true knowledge of God as verified in the Word made flesh.

[6] *Ibid.*

III

KNOWLEDGE AND PRETENSE BY THE FALSE TEACHERS

2:1-22

Having presented his witnesses, Peter proceeds in chapter 2, to strip the false teachers of all pretense and to display them in their true light. Analyzing their program, he proceeds to build his case by probing their motives and rationale and concludes with a brief of their just desert.

A. THE PROGRAM ANALYZED, 2:1-10a

1. *Their Presence, 1a*

The Christians addressed in Peter's second epistle need not be under a misapprehension regarding the presence of evil workers in their midst. It may afford little comfort, but it is certainly helpful to know that false prophets have always tried to work deceit among the chosen of God; New Testament saints were not immune. Deceivers coming into the midst "prophesy lies" out of deceitful hearts while pretending to speak in the name of the Lord (Jer. 14:14).

2. *Their Position, 1b*

By stealth and deception they bring in "destructive heresies" (ASV) which, once implanted, spawn an evil brood of immoral practices. These deceivers live and act only for themselves, with no thought for God's holiness and their personal accountability. They "choose the name of Christ to call themselves by, but cast aside the doctrine of the Cross both in its discipline for their lives, and as the altar of human redemption."[1]

As the culmination of their unbelief, they deny "the Master that bought them" (ASV). Peter knew what it was to deny Christ in a moment of weakness (Matt. 26:70). He also knew the exercise of a repentant heart, the relief of forgiveness and the joy of restored fellowship. But with the false teachers there was no sensitivity. Denial was an established mode of life, evidenced by word and practice.

Some may find irreconcilable the fact of their denial and that Christ had bought them. These two lines of thought become clear when cast in

[1] J. Rawson Lumby, "The Epistles of St. Peter," *The Expositor's Bible* (New York: A. C. Armstrong & Son, 1908), p. 285.

the light of the analogy of master and slave. He
who purchases a slave has complete ownership
because the price has been paid, but the slave
may rebel and disavow the transaction, even to
desertion. The Master (*despotēs*, signifying complete ownership and mastery) paid the full price
of their redemption (I Peter 1:18-19), but these
heretics are insensitive to everything except carnal appetites which they determine to satisfy at
any cost.

3. *Their Persuasiveness, 2-3a*

Strangely enough, their ranks are swelled with
a following not from paganism but from the
church. The peddlers of heresy gain a following
primarily because their message gives license to
the flesh rather than calling for its crucifixion.

Because of licentious practices in the lives of
some who profess to be Christian, many non-
Christians pass judgment on the Christian way of
life, calling it undisciplined and immoral. This
brings reproach upon the cause of Christ.

The false prophets persuade many who are
unstable to follow their evil ways by using
"feigned words." The New English Bible speaks of
their "sheer fabrications." (*Plastos* means "mould-
ed as from clay." See Romans 9:20.) Covetousness
is the deceivers' motivation, the only motivation

compatible with their evil designs. Their method of operation is making merchandise of unsuspecting Christians.

4. *Their Perdition, 3b-10a*

While judgment of the deceivers may be long in coming, the consummation is certain because God has already judged their actions. The words of Lowell, "Truth forever on the scaffold, Wrong forever on the throne," so often taunt the believer's mind. Yet "behind the dim unknown, Standeth God within the shadow, keeping watch upon His own" ("The Present Crisis"). In His own good time His judgment will be made manifest for all to behold.

Pride, so obvious in these false teachers, is only a "prelude to their fall," illustrated so forcefully in God's judgment upon the angels that sinned. Disobedience cannot be tolerated and will be judged as it was in Noah's day. Sensuality has a grim memorial to its just judgment in the charred ruins of Sodom and Gomorrah.[2]

In the three examples of verses 4-9, Peter aptly characterizes the perverters of truth. He says that their impending judgment is with the same certainty and finality of the Old Testament examples.

[2] *Ibid.,* pp. 288-89.

Because of pride, 4. Judgment upon sinning angels is alluded to in Jude 6. "And the angels which kept not their first estate, but left their own habitation, He [God] hath reserved . . . unto the judgment." These were creatures who stood in God's presence but were cast down to hell because of their sin. The word used here is *Tartarus* which in early Christian writings seemed to designate the prison or abode in the nether world where fallen angels were kept until the final judgment. It indicates the deepest abyss of the nether world and is so used in the apocryphal book of Enoch (20:2). In contrast, the term *Gehenna* is used to designate the place where the spirits of apostate Jews were kept.

Because of disobedience, 5. The world of Noah's day was characterized by an utter disregard for the preaching of righteousness and chose to go in the way of the flesh. It is worthy of note that in Genesis 6:5-7 the wickedness of man is given as the occasion for judgment. In Matthew 24:38 Jesus commented on their total absorption with the natural and utter disregard of the supernatural.

Because of sensuality, 6-10a. Destruction of the five cities of the plain, particularly Sodom and Gomorrah, stands as "an object-lesson for godless men in future days" (New English Bible). God is

no respecter of favored positions among men. The
cities were advanced in civilization and located
on a fertile, well-watered plain. Prosperous according to every measure of man, they still did
not escape God's judgment. However, God delivered *just* Lot out of the midst before judgment
fell.

In the examples pertaining to man, God's grace
is clearly intermingled with His justice, particularly in Lot's case. The historical accounting in
Genesis does not place Lot in too favorable a
light. He had to be forced out of Sodom; he later
became drunk and sired sons by his two daugh-
ters.

But the appraisal given in this epistle calls him
"just Lot, vexed with the filthy conversation of the
wicked," and "that righteous man dwelling
among them, in seeing and hearing, vexed his
righteous soul from day to day with their unlaw-
ful deeds." This description of Lot has been most
comforting to the righteous remnant of all generations in times when evil threatens. Therefore, it
is clearly demonstrated that "the Lord knoweth
how to deliver the godly out of temptations," and
surely in wrath He remembers mercy.

B. THE PHILOSOPHY SCRUTINIZED, 2:10*b*-19

Peter's presentation of the case against these

reprobates is perceptive, terse and unmitigated. It moves swiftly to a conclusion at the end of the chapter, leaving no room for doubt as to the Holy Spirit's appraisal of these lustful, self-appointed leaders. Most effectively they are described as lacking the virtues one expects to find in a leader. They are the spiritual "have-nots," by choice not circumstance. Hence they are devoid of any awareness of spiritual dimensions to life; they are devoid of self-control, giving free rein to their lusts; they are devoid of self-respect because they are "slaves of corruption" (RSV).

1. *Spiritually Insensitive,* 10*b*-13*a*

This insensitivity has its source in their animal-like nature, knowing only the law of self-preservation, experiencing satisfaction only in carnal indulgences. (In verse 12 they are called "creatures without reason" and "mere animals.")

Because the reality, even existence, of a spiritual realm is absolutely foreign to them, not even the supernatural escapes their railing. In all probability, evil angels ("dignities") are in view because in verse 11 the apostle says that even angels, "greater in might and power," dare not pronounce "a railing judgment against them before the Lord." Yet these revile "in matters whereof they are ignorant" (ASV).

2. *Sensually Incited,* 13b-16

The word picture Peter paints is anything but flattering. The reprobates have a greedy appetite that feeds on every form of sensual pleasure but is never satisfied. Their only purpose in associating with the unstable Christian is to wean him away for the satisfaction of fleshly lusts. Because they have their "hearts trained in greed" (RSV), everything that issues from their hearts is directed toward gratification of fleshly lusts. (See Proverbs 4:23; 23:7.) Therefore the members obey the dictates of the heart with "eyes full of adultery" and feet that follow "the way of Balaam." (This reminds one of the description of Israel's backslidden state, recorded in Isaiah 1:5-6.)

Peter likens them to Balaam who "loved the wages of unrighteousness"—a most interesting analogy. To serve the ends of Balak, king of Moab, Balaam had hired out his prophetic gift against the wandering Israelites. So the Jewish nation was cursed by the prophet, but he himself was rebuked by God. Balaam's sensual deed stands as a reminder of God's judgment upon all who would prostitute God-given talents and gifts for sake of gain.

3. *Subtly Impelled,* 17-19

These false teachers made a loud and convincing profession of being champions of fulfillment and heralds of freedom. But in reality, this profession was only empty prattle ("great swelling words of vanity"). No correspondence can be found between what they profess and what they are in nature and practice.

With the subtlety of Satan himself, these men were enticing, promising satisfaction and fulfillment of natural appetites. Many of those caught were unstable and immature believers—those "who are just escaping from them that live in error" (a more accurate rendering of the Greek in v. 18). The deceivers justified such action under the guise of "liberty," freeing weaker Christians from the legalism to which the more devout had subjected themselves.

Peter likens the false teachers to "springs without water, and mists driven by a storm" (ASV). (See also Jude's description of them.) To people utterly dependent on nature's own supply of refreshment for sustaining life, these figures of speech were most graphic—springs which yielded no water, and mists that should produce rain, driven away by strong winds.

The irony is that these false teachers are "bondservants of corruption" (ASV), being hopelessly chained by the very practices they encourage in immature Christians.

C. THE PENALTY SUMMARIZED, 2:20-22

1. *The Predicament*, 20

Whether Peter has in mind the deceivers or the deceived is not clear from the wording of the texts but the principle stated would apply equally to both. In describing the threat to the church, the apostle does not concern himself with God's purpose in election nor yet with eternal salvation. Peter's concern is for those whom he loves in the faith and he makes it very clear that these false teachers are not good examples to follow.

The state described in verse 20 is the result of giving way to the allurement of lusts and passions, even after one has been delivered through the full knowledge (*epignōsis*) of the Lord and Saviour Jesus Christ. Experiencing such deliverance, it is difficult to understand how one could return to the old life. This condition is similar to that described in Matthew 12:43-45 and Hebrews 6:4-6.

2. *The Proposition*, 21

What has taken place cannot be undone, but for the apostates, it would have been better never to have known the "way of righteousness." This undoubtedly refers to their destructive, sacrilegious influence, more insidious because many

sacred things of God's revelation to man have
been made known to them. The "holy commandment" probably refers to the truth of God as
revealed in Jesus Christ. (See also 2:2.)

3. *The Proverb*, 22

Peter illustrates the disgusting, pitiable state of
these apostates by pointing to two Oriental
scavengers, dogs and swine, both unclean by the
dietary laws of the Old Covenant. More telling
examples of debauchery and insensitivity would
have been difficult to find and certainly such individuals can be neither examples nor teachers.

IV

KNOWLEDGE AND PERCEPTION THROUGH REVELATION
3:1—18*a*

Any knowledge possessed by the false teachers makes them only more hardened to spiritual verities and a greater threat to young Christians. Contrariwise, knowledge perceived by a sincere heart, even on the part of a new believer, leads to a clearer understanding of God's love, His purpose in grace, and His revelation to man.

The apostle concludes his epistle by extolling the Word of God proven by experience and visibly demonstrated in history. This is done with cogent arguments for the need of personal growth, the utter reliability of witnesses to Christ's majesty, and the dangers posed by false prophets in their midst.

A. CERTITUDE OF GOD'S SPOKEN WORD, 3:1-7

Although the apostates ignore God's chastening and judgment, He has promised that judgment

for disobedience is inevitable and will come when
least expected. This is now the "second epistle"
which Peter had written (the first being, in all
probability, I Peter); and his chief concern is to
bring to mind what God has said as opposed to
the words of false teachers which lead only to
spiritual dearth.

1. *By Reflection,* 1-2

Here the apostle does not try to reveal some-
thing new but does try to cause the readers to
reflect on things which were told them by the
apostles. How strange that the readers forgot so
soon or were weaned away from the words of life.

This letter is an attempt to stir up their pure,
yet forgetful, minds to draw strength and life
from the message (cf. 1:13). Their minds are
characterized as "pure." (Plato used this word for
"ethical purity."[1]) But their minds need stirring up
and their powers of recall need sharpening. If
successful, truth would become their shield and
buckler against erroneous teachings and practices. Furthermore, their eyes would be lifted
from the here and now to end-time events when
God would vindicate His word by judging the
ungodly and receiving the redeemed into the
eternal state of blessedness.

[1] Archibald T. Robertson, *Word Pictures in the New Testament* (Nashville: Broadman Press, 1933), VI, 172.

2. *By Reaction*, 3-4

While the believer should respond gladly to all that God has spoken, the ungodly react much differently, as one might expect.

Scoffing. These scoffers attempt to discredit God's word as Satan did in the garden by casting doubt on the veracity of His promises. If the authority of the Bible is undermined, then "what can the righteous do?" (Ps. 11:3). A foundation, a good foundation, is a necessity in building, whether it be an imposing edifice or a godly life.

The coming of scoffers is certain. Twice Peter speaks of their presence, in 2:1 and 3:3, and both times in the future tense. They are "mockers with mockery," parading their esoteric knowledge as the truth. The Christian, being forewarned, is thereby safeguarded against intellectual and moral bondage to a lustful system that erodes the very foundations of the faith. Thus freed from bondage, the Christian can enjoy this present life with no fear of impending judgment.

The Septuagint Version of Isaiah 3:4 gives a graphic picture, shedding light on this passage. Impending judgment is the prophet's great burden. God, he announces, will remove the men of mature wisdom and experience in all areas of life and in their stead children and babies shall rule.

The word used for mocking is the same used in
Isaiah to mean "playing like children."[2]

Skepticism. In questioning "the promise of his
coming" these scoffers make three assumptions
which lead them far from the truth. First, they
assume that their knowledge of historical events is
full and complete and that if there had been
divine intervention in the history of mankind they
would know of it.

Second, they assume that history is complete
and accurate. Yet, strangely enough, the more
that modern scholars engage in research, the more
they realize that history is not replete nor is it free
of bias and prejudices.

The third assumption, and perhaps the most
misleading, is that they reckon on the absolute
uniformity of nature. Uniformity certainly characterizes the natural creation, otherwise there
would be *chaos* rather than *cosmos*—"an orderly
harmonious systematic universe." It is only because God has established the universe and set in
operation laws to control and govern it that scien-
tific investigation in all realms of life is possible.

Many modern scholars, recognizing only the
laws and not the "Lawgiver" (of natural laws),
feel that determination of future events is inherent in the "laws" and not in any supposed Creator

2 *Ibid.,* p. 173.

who established these laws of operation. In this is seen the primary difference between natural philosophy and Christian (or theistic) philosophy. The latter says that there is a Creator, absolute, transcendent and self-sufficient, who established the universe. At will He is able to intervene in the outworking of these laws or even to bring about complete destruction.

Over 1900 years ago God stepped into the stream of history in the person of Christ, and His second coming is as certain as the well-attested fact of the incarnation. Let the scoffers be true to their presuppositions of unbelief! For the true believer scoffing will not alter the hope or reality of His promised return.

3. *By Recount*, 5-7

The best antidote for doubt or flagging faith is to recount experiences of God's faithfulness in behalf of His Creation. To illustrate, Peter points out three creative activities of the Word of God.

Creation, 5. In Genesis 1 creation is the result of God's spoken word of command. Seven times in the six creative days we read, "God said, Let there be . . . ," and one by one the facets of creation were manifested. It was "by the word of God" that "the world was created" (Heb. 11:3). But this fact is understood only by men of faith.

Judgment, 6. The flood of Noah's day cannot be ignored, neither as a historic fact nor as a cogent argument for God's intervention in the operation of divinely established laws. It was by "the word" of God that judgment fell. "Whereby" translates an expression which is literally "through which," a plural pronoun, undoubtedly referring back to the antecedents "word of God" and "water" in verse 5. Hence, God's word initiated the judgment even as He had spoken through Noah's preaching.

Preservation, 7. With dissipation of energy, propensity to decay, deterioration and disease culminating in death, man's best efforts can do but little to preserve the natural order. But God by that "same word," active in creation and in judgment, is withholding judgment for the heavens and the earth—judgment that is inevitable because of sin. He has kept His creation "in store" until the judgment of "ungodly men." God has spoken and all His pronouncements shall be fulfilled.

B. CONFIDENCE IN GOD'S PROMISED WORD, 3:8-13

How often the Christian becomes weary and is prone to doubt God because things taken by faith do not readily materialize. At these times it cannot be forgotten that man is a mortal creature and bound by limits of time and space. God, who is eternal and transcendent, does not work as man might expect or even hope. (See Isa. 55:8-9.) Therefore, the believer rests with confidence on the promises of the heavenly Father.

1. *Because of His Patience*, 8-9

Peter uses the words of Psalm 90, "a prayer of Moses," to impress upon his readers the reason for God's patient dealings with man in his sin and unbelief. "A thousand years in thy sight are but as yesterday when it is past" (v. 4). "St. Peter not only adopts, but adapts, the words for his own purpose."[3]

This cannot be construed as a standard by which God works in time, nor can it be used as a key for interpreting all temporal references in prophecy. Because Peter equates a thousand years as one day and one day as a thousand years, it is quite obvious he is clearly saying that God recognizes no temporal measure for the out-working of His purposes. It has been said that with God there is no time—past, present or future—but one eternal now. Hence, speaking after

[3] J. Rawson Lumby, "The Epistles of St. Peter," *The Expositor's Bible* (New York: A. C. Armstrong & Son, 1908), p. 345.

the manner of men, God can afford to be patient.

The apostles expected Christ to return in their lifetime and shared this hope with the early church. His longsuffering with man in his sinful ways has spanned more than nineteen hundred years, although the door of grace could have been closed at any time. The primary reason is clear in the text—"that all should come to repentance."

2. *Because of His Provision,* 10-13

The future is dark indeed for the "ungodly men" (v. 7) and the "but" introducing verse 10 ties that which follows to the statement of verse 7 as a conclusion. Judgment has been withheld but the "day of the Lord" will come. Twice in this context the "day" is mentioned and in the second reference the term "the day of God" is used.

While there has been much discussion of these two terms in theological circles, the meanings seem quite obvious. Rather than referring to two different periods, each with its own significance, these terms simply refer to that time when God sets His hand to consummate sin and wickedness, bringing to an end the day of man. Adding to the awesomeness of this judgment is the suddenness with which it breaks around the unbelieving—"as a thief in the night." This metaphor is not unique to Peter but is rather common in the New Testament, representing unexpected and undesired arrival (Matt. 24:43; Luke 12:39; I Thess. 5:2; Rev. 3:3; 16:15).

God's provision for His own is clearer when contrasted with the judgment from which they are delivered. In verse 10 the two areas of judgment are mentioned—heavens and earth. "Elements" refers to the "building blocks" from which the heavens and earth are made, the Greek word connoting an orderly, regimented arrangement. These "elements shall melt with fervent heat." The cause of this disintegration is expressed by a word commonly used of a fever. This use causes Mayor to suggest that the burning mentioned here is caused by internal heat.[4] To those living in this age of atomic fission, such a concept is not difficult to grasp.

With the "loosing" or "liquefying" (literal translations of the words used in verses 10 and 12) of the elements, the passing away of both heaven and earth is a logical consequence. The heavens shall pass away with a "great noise." Writers of the last century expressed it by the ideas of a whizzing arrow, thunder, the crash of devouring flames. A contemporary, J. B. Phillips, uses "a terrific tearing blast." Today those who know the

[4] Robertson, *op. cit.*, p. 176.

destructive potential of nuclear stockpiles throughout the world can best approximate, with tormented imagination, the situation Peter describes here.

The earth shall be "burned up." That for which men labor a lifetime, only to die and leave it to others, shall pass away. Material security in which men trust shall be removed as things that can be shaken (Heb. 12:27). Judgment must purge as far as the taint of sin has reached. Only thus can God provide a new order for the redeemed.

Exercised by contemplation of God's judgment, the believer is sobered and challenged in renewed dedication to a life of true holiness. In this world, now under impending judgment, the believer is not in his native element but is a stranger and pilgrim. In the new order which God has promised, righteousness "shall be at home." Then those who are righteousness (I Cor. 1:30; II Cor. 5:21) shall no longer be a despised minority but shall discover that they alone have titular rights in the new heavens and new earth.

C. COMMITMENT TO GOD'S WRITTEN WORD, 3:14-18*a*

Peter desires that his spiritual charges heed the things he has written, things intended to keep them "without spot and blameless." Such commitment fosters in the Christian a proper attitude toward God's purpose in redemption and leads to attainment of all He in grace has provided.

1. *In Attitude,* 14-16

In light of all that God has just revealed through His prophet, the Christian should desire above all else to be acceptable to God and to show forth the fruits of salvation. Peter had written out of great burden because of the urgent need and the issues at stake.

But then he was not the only one communicating this same burden to the young churches. Paul too had written in a similar vein and many would misunderstand and misconstrue Peter's words as they had Paul's. Whether it be the writings of Peter or of Paul, both present the common theme of redemption; and the true believer's attitude toward that message is characterized by acceptance of its authority and patient waiting for its fulfillment.

Not all who heard shared that attitude, especially toward Paul's letters. It was not Pauline authorship nor yet the degree of inspiration which caused the difficulty. (These letters had not at that time been brought to the dissecting table of the destructive critics.) Some "unlearned and unstable" readers twisted and misapplied the letters; so that which was meant to impart life opened the door to destruction (cf. 2:21).

Several facts emerge concerning acceptance and esteem of Pauline epistles at the time of Peter's writing, c. 66-67 A.D.: they were written by Paul out of a supply of divine wisdom; there were a number of letters extant by that time ("all his epistles," although not necessarily all that are present today); Paul's letters are identified as Scripture equally with the Old Testament books, implied in the words "other scriptures."

2. *In Attainment*, 17-18a

The informed Christian had no excuse for stopping short in attainment of all God provided for maturity and stability. By the inspired writings they had been exhorted to godly living, to a knowledge which comes from God only, and to a hope transcending all human difficulties. The passions and pitfalls leading to bondage and blindness cannot enslave the informed Christian who has learned to rely on God's grace and to counter reasonings of men with the true knowledge of Him who is both Saviour from sin and Lord of life. To this end is the Word of the living God recorded in Scripture.

V

BENEDICTION

3:18*b*

The benediction is in keeping with the accepted style of letter-writing but is quite different. It is nonetheless meaningful, especially in light of the immediate context. He who is both Saviour and Lord deserves all praise and glory, beginning now in the host of the redeemed and swelling to a universal paean of praise throughout all ages.

BIBLIOGRAPHY

COMMENTARIES

ALFORD, HENRY. *The Greek New Testament*, Vol. IV. Chicago: Moody Press, 1958.

AUGUSTINUS, AURELIUS. *The Confessions* (*Basic Writings*), Vol. I. Edited by WHITNEY J. OATES, New York: Random House Publishers, 1948.

BEARE, FRANCIS WRIGHT. *The First Epistle of Peter*. Oxford: Basil Blackwell, 1947.

FERRIN, HOWARD W. *Strengthen Thy Brethren*. Grand Rapids: Zondervan Publishing House, 1942.

HOMRIGHAUSEN, ELMER G. *The Interpreter's Bible*, Vol. XII. New York and Nashville: Abingdon Press, 1955.

HUNTER, ARCHIBALD M. *The Interpreter's Bible*, Vol. XII. New York and Nashville: Abingdon Press, 1955.

JOWETT, J. H. *The Redeemed Family of God*. New York: George H. Doran Co., 1906.

LENSKI, R. C. H. *The Interpretation of the Epistles of St. Peter, St. John and St. Jude*. Columbus, Ohio: Lutheran Book Concern, 1938.

LUMBY, J. RAWSON. "The Epistles of St. Peter." *The Expositor's Bible*. New York: A. C. Armstrong & Son, 1908.

MAYCOCK, EDWARD A. *A Letter of Wise Counsel.* (World Christian Books, No. 15.) London: Lutterworth Press, 1957.

MEYER, F. B. *Tried by Fire.* New York: Fleming H. Revell Co., n.d.

ROBERTSON, ARCHIBALD T. *Word Pictures in the New Testament, Vol. VI.* Nashville: Broadman Press, 1933.

SELWYN, EDWARD G. *The First Epistle of St. Peter.* London: Macmillan & Co., Ltd., 1964.

TENNEY, MERRILL C. *The New Testament.* Grand Rapids: Wm. B. Eerdmans Publishing Co., 1953.

GENERAL REFERENCE WORKS

Ante-Nicene Christian Library, Translations of the Writings of the Fathers down to A.D. 325. Edited by ALEXANDER ROBERTS and JAMES DONALDSON. 24 vols. Edinburgh: T. & T. Clark, 1870.

ARNDT, WILLIAM F., and GINGRICH, F. WILBUR. A *Greek-English Lexicon of the New Testament.* Chicago: University of Chicago Press, 1957.

ORR, JAMES (ed.). "The Temple," *The International Standard Bible Encyclopaedia,* Vol. V. Grand Rapids: Wm. B. Eerdmans Publishing Co., 1947.